MICHIGAN'S
STRYCHNINE SAINT

MICHIGAN'S
STRYCHNINE SAINT

THE CURIOUS CASE OF MRS. MARY McKNIGHT

TOBIN T. BUHK

THE
History
PRESS

Published by The History Press
Charleston, SC 29403
www.historypress.net

Copyright © 2014 by Tobin T. Buhk
All rights reserved

First published 2014

Manufactured in the United States

ISBN 978.1.62619.257.7

Library of Congress CIP data applied for.

Contents

Contents

Acknowledgements

Writing a book is a true labor of love but one not possible without the gracious help and support of others.

In particular, I would like to thank Jennifer Richmond for her help in tracking down old prisoner records in Detroit; Fel Brunett, historian and curator of the Fife Lake Museum, for his help in obtaining images of early twentieth-century Fife Lake; and Lisa Leach, secretary of the board of directors of the Fife Lake Historical Society, for her assistance in tracing the Murphy family tree and supplying several unique images for this text. Lisa's input on Murphy family genealogy and her insight into Mary McKnight's past were not only vital to this work but also inspirational. From locating a copy of the mysterious mortgage document to shooting a few photographs of Murphy family headstones (two of which appear in this volume), Lisa has provided invaluable research on the subject.

Breathing life into long-gone characters is no easy task. While every effort has been made to ensure the following text is historically accurate to a *T*, the occasional slip up sometimes occurs. If there are any unintended errors, they are mine and mine alone.

What you are about to read is a true story, unembellished by fictionalized dialogue or other window dressings of the novelist.

Introduction

SPRINGFIELD CEMETERY, SPRINGFIELD TOWNSHIP, MICHIGAN[1]
Wednesday, June 3, 1903

John Jors, sexton of the Springfield Cemetery, stared at the headstone of Gertrude Murphy as the diggers began skinning the grass beside her marker. The tombstone contained just one name, but the sexton knew that the grave held two bodies: a mother and daughter who died tragically just an hour apart on April 20.

Jors ran his hand across the smooth marble and eyed the bare earth covering the adjacent grave site. Just five days earlier, they had unearthed that grave. The exhumation led to disturbing questions, and the county prosecutor hoped to find the answers in Gertrude Murphy's coffin.

Within an hour, the gravediggers had removed the topsoil and created a trench about seven feet in length. They stood waist deep in the hole and tossed out shovels of dirt as they burrowed their way deeper. The earth was loose and easy to move, so it wouldn't take them much longer to reach the coffin about three feet below.

Sheriff John W. Creighton stood at the edge of the grass and peered into the trench. Creighton felt a knot in his stomach. He massaged the bridge of his nose with his thumb and forefinger, while Kalkaska County prosecutor Ernest C. Smith anxiously shifted his weight from one foot to another. Dr. Perly W. Pearsall, a local physician, thumbed through his bag for the scalpel he would

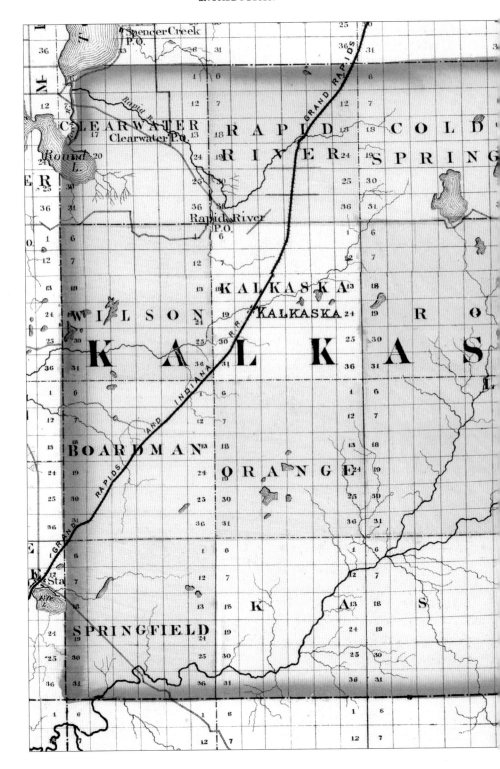

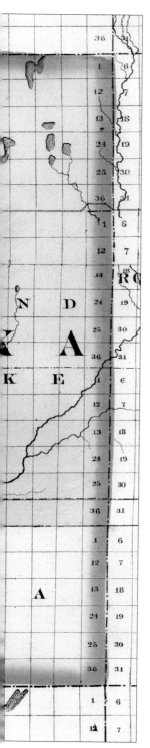

use to remove the stomachs of both bodies. Smith would then take the organs to a chemist in Ann Arbor. Jors crossed his arms and watched the men work.

Until a few weeks ago, none of them had witnessed an exhumation; now, they were on their second in a week.

Although Jors understood the necessity for the spadework, he felt a sense of uneasiness. Unlike the first grave they had unearthed a few days earlier, this one contained two corpses: a child—Ruth Murphy—buried in the arms of her mother, Gertrude. Jors remembered vividly the wake and the open casket in which the mother held her precious daughter in one final, everlasting embrace.

Now, a month later, the earth would disgorge a ghastly sight. Two bodies withered by decomposition, the white silk lining of the coffin stained by the body fluids that caused their torsos to bloat and then burst. It was the natural way of death, but it was also an ugly process that people kept hidden in caskets beneath layers of earth. Yet in this case, Smith and Creighton couldn't let the dead rest in peace.

Map of Kalkaska County from the *H.F. Walling Atlas*, published in 1873. The Murphy family lived in section 21 of Springfield Township at the southwest corner of the county. Fife Lake is just across the county line, in Grand Traverse County. *Author's collection.*

Part 1

Death Suits Her

1
The Wake

Wednesday, April 22, 1903

Carriages lined the dirt road leading to a small white two-story house as relatives came to pay their last respects to Isaiah "John" Murphy's twenty-two-year-old bride, Gertrude, and their three-month-old daughter, Ruth.[2] The young couple had moved in with John's sixty-six-year-old mother, Sarah, while they put the finishing touches on a new home on a nearby forty-acre parcel of land. John's widowed sister, Mary (Murphy) McKnight, and cousin Mary Mullen also lived with Sarah Murphy.

Two days earlier—on April 20—Gertrude had gone to work at the new house and left Ruth in the care of Mary McKnight. Aunt Mary tucked Ruth into her crib for an afternoon nap. A few hours later, she went to check on the baby and found an appalling sight: Ruth, her skin baby-blue, lay motionless. She had apparently become entangled in the soft bed linen and suffocated.

Gertrude returned around lunchtime. When Mary broke the news about Ruth, she flew into hysterics, wildly gesturing, pacing back and forth and mumbling incoherent ramblings in between loud shrieks. Once Sarah and Mary managed to calm Gertrude, John went to Fife Lake to purchase a coffin from the undertaker Willis Brower.[3]

While he was gone, Gertrude became suddenly ill. She complained of a neck ache and shivered as if she had the grip. Then she experienced a violent

W. W. BROWER

Funeral Director _____

Fine Burial Caskets,
All styles of Robes,
We do Embalming.

All calls, day or night,
attended to promptly.
We are fully equipped to
render first-class service.

Above: Fife Lake, circa 1900. Willis Brower's store and mortuary is the brick building behind the bandstand. His brother, E.C. Brower, owned the store in the foreground. While John Murphy traveled to Fife Lake to purchase a coffin for his daughter, Ruth, his wife, Gertrude, mysteriously died. *Fife Lake Historical Society.*

Left: Advertisement for Brower's undertaking services published in an 1896 edition of the *Fife Lake Monitor. Collection of Lisa Leach.*

convulsion. Her body twitched spasmodically; she foamed at the mouth and threw her head back. Her lips were drawn, exposing her teeth and forming a sinister expression, like she had just seen a demon. She clenched her fists so tightly they turned white, and her balled hands snapped up toward her chest like some malignant puppeteer had yanked strings attached to her arms. The convulsion lasted for a few painful minutes, and then her body appeared to relax, her hands opening and dropping to her sides.

Mary McKnight, who witnessed the terrifying spectacle, had just managed to catch her breath when Gertrude's body began to twitch again. The convulsions came in waves, and she suffered from several more before she stopped moving. Her death occurred with shocking swiftness; she was gone within twenty minutes of the first episode and just an hour after her daughter.[4]

The next morning, Dr. S.E. Neihardt made the trip from South Boardman. After listening to family members describe the symptoms, he concluded that Gertrude died from shock following an epileptic fit. Ruth, he wrote on the official death certificate, died following "spasms." The puzzled doctor didn't list an "immediate cause of death" or a "disease causing death" on the official paperwork.[5]

Ruth and Gertrude Murphy would share a funeral and a coffin.

The Murphy women had prepared the house for a traditional Irish wake. They reversed a large oval mirror that hung on one wall of the parlor, and they stopped the hands of the grandfather clock. The casket was placed in the center of the room, where John stood by the side of his deceased wife. John Murphy glanced at the coffin containing his family. Gertrude held their baby in her arms. They almost looked like they were asleep, as if he could nudge them and they would wake. Gertrude even appeared to be slightly grinning in her slumber.

Sarah Murphy sat in a chair next to her son John and watched as her friends and relatives began filling the room. Men dressed in their best Sunday attire escorted women in black mourning dresses fringed with taffeta and lace.

Thirty-five years of carving out a place in the wilderness had taken their toll on the Murphy matriarch. Stooped over from an arthritic spine, she walked with a slight limp.

In 1870, she and her husband, Isiah, emigrated from Canada and settled in northern Michigan. Isiah worked in the lumber camps during the winter months and tilled a tract of land in the spring and summer. Together, they had five sons and four daughters. Already, the family plot contained the graves of two Murphy children, and the next day, it would grow larger with the addition of a daughter-in-law and a grandchild.

Most of the mourners understood John Murphy's pain. They all knew someone who had passed away unexpectedly. Hewing out a living from the area's forests was difficult labor and dangerous for northern Michigan's pioneer families. Accidents and disease claimed lives every year, but the Murphy family had endured more than their share of tragedy. Some even said they were cursed. Sarah and Isiah Murphy lost their eighteen-year-old daughter, Sarah, to unknown causes in 1894. Later that same year, Isiah passed away.

On December 3, 1902, Willie Murphy was killed in a tragic hunting accident. While Willie was walking through Maple Forest Township in Crawford County, a local named Asa Valentine mistook him for a deer. Valentine's shot struck Willie in the throat, tearing through his neck and spine. Paralyzed, he crumpled to the ground and screamed for help.

Valentine followed the screams and found Willie, motionless, in a heap. He ran for help, but by the time he returned, twenty-one-year-old William Murphy was dead. Ironically, the *Grayling Avalanche* noted in its December 3 article about the accident that "Murphy was afraid of the fool hunters who infest the woods and had put on a red sweater for protection."[6] The wake took place just a few weeks before the family celebrated Christmas.

Mary Mullen stood next to Sarah, holding her hand. The twenty-eight-year-old adored Mama Murphy, who looked after her as a mother would. Sarah always shook a stick at people who mocked Mary or called her "touched."

Mary McKnight also stood next to Sarah. She knew, perhaps more than anyone in the room, the pain John felt with the passing of Gertrude and Ruth. She had lost both of her husbands and all five of her children. Three died in infancy and two died of diphtheria before they reached the age of five.

Gertrude's father and mother—Anson and Mary Ward—made the trip from Otsego Lake to say goodbye to their eldest child. Mary Ward shrieked when she saw Gertrude in the casket at the front of the parlor. She fell to her knees and began to sob. Anson put his hand on her trembling shoulder and thought of Gertrude's wedding day. It seemed like just yesterday he had given his daughter away in marriage, and she was so happy.

After a brief pause, Anson led his wife to where John stood. Mary Ward threw her arms around her son-in-law and kissed him on the cheek.

John's eldest brother, James Murphy, escorted his wife, Jennie, to the front of the parlor, where they both knelt and whispered a prayer. James and Jennie lived in Crawford County, where James worked a spread of land while Jennie looked after their three children. Just a little over a year earlier, they had lost their daughter Fern to scarlet fever.

Sarah Murphy squeezed John's hand when she noticed his younger brothers Danny and Charley enter the parlor. Danny Murphy walked over to the coffin, got down on one knee and muttered a prayer before approaching his brother. Overcome with emotion, he hugged John. Charley followed Danny's lead, first offering a prayer and then greeting John at the reception line.

Bracing herself on her husband's (William) arm, John's older sister Margaret (Murphy) Chalker approached the coffin. She gasped when she saw the baby in Gertrude's arms and covered her face with a gloved hand. William Chalker wrapped his arm around her waist and led her to John.

Tears rolled down her cheeks as she embraced him. Johnny always looked after her and her sisters, and when Papa died, he had become the head of the family at twenty-four. Like her mother, Margaret knew the range of emotions John would experience in the coming months: an overwhelming sense of despair and hopelessness followed by an empty, hollow feeling. In 1893, her daughter Eliza had become ill after afternoon tea with Aunt Mary McKnight. She suffered from several seizures before she died.

Margaret unclenched her arms from John's neck. Her husband handed her a handkerchief, which she used to dry her cheeks, and they joined her brothers in the back of the parlor.

As Margaret moved toward the back of the room, her younger sister Martha (Murphy) Woodard and her husband, Jerome, approached the casket. After a brief prayer, Martha whispered something in John's ear before joining the others.

Dr. Perly W. Pearsall, with his wife, Adella, by his side, followed the Woodards. Dr. Pearsall had known the family for years, making periodic house calls from his Fife Lake office. When he visited the Murphy place on the afternoon Gertrude died, Sarah Murphy had escorted him to the upstairs room, where he found Gertrude's body sprawled out on the bed.

The position of her body indicated the agony she suffered in her last few minutes of life. Her still-clenched fists were pulled up to her chest, and the froth at the corners of her mouth had turned into an off-white crust. Pearsall thought that Gertrude suffered from an epileptic fit, but one thing particularly bothered him: Gertrude's limbs hadn't become flaccid before rigor mortis set in. They remained rigid in the hours immediately after her death as if frozen in some battle with an unknown enemy. He knew that a violent seizure could cause a rapid onset of rigor mortis, but the description

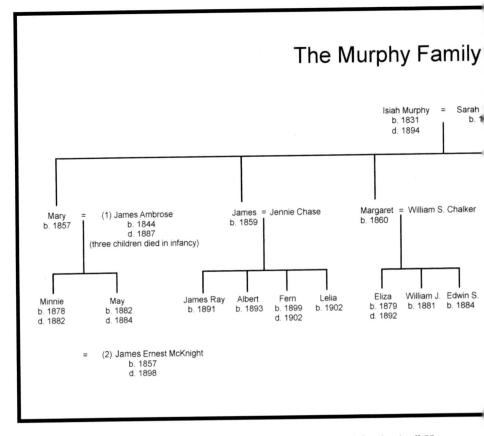

The Murphy Family

Isiah Murphy = Sarah
b. 1831   b. 1
d. 1894

Mary = (1) James Ambrose   James = Jennie Chase   Margaret = William S. Chalker
b. 1857   b. 1844   b. 1859   b. 1860
             d. 1887
        (three children died in infancy)

Minnie   May   James Ray   Albert   Fern   Lelia   Eliza   William J. Edwin S.
b. 1878   b. 1882   b. 1891   b. 1893   b. 1899   b. 1902   b. 1879   b. 1881   b. 1884
d. 1882   d. 1884   d. 1902   d. 1892

= (2) James Ernest McKnight
       b. 1857
       d. 1898

The Murphy family tree on the day of the wake for Gertrude and Ruth Murphy, April 22, 1903. *Courtesy of the author.*

of Gertrude's convulsions didn't sound like other epileptic seizures that Pearsall had witnessed. He was left with a vague sense that something wasn't quite right.

Unlike the other mourners, Pearsall paused at the coffin. The undertaker did excellent work, he thought as he recalled the strange conversation he'd had with William Wilson, who helped embalm the bodies in preparation for the wake.[7] Wilson remarked that Gertrude's limbs were so stiff he had to push with all his strength just to straighten them. Pearsall shook his head and approached the grief-stricken husband. He grasped John's hand and held it for a few moments.

Joe Battenfield followed Dr. Pearsall. Battenfield lived about a quarter of a mile away from the Murphy farm. He had known the family for over twenty

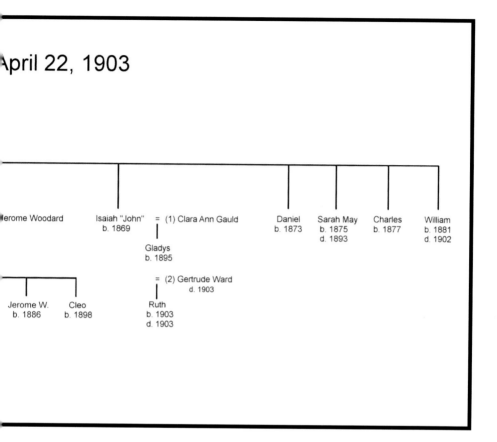

April 22, 1903

Jerome Woodard

Isaiah "John"
b. 1869

= (1) Clara Ann Gauld

Gladys
b. 1895

= (2) Gertrude Ward
d. 1903

Daniel
b. 1873

Sarah May
b. 1875
d. 1893

Charles
b. 1877

William
b. 1881
d. 1902

Jerome W.
b. 1886

Cleo
b. 1898

Ruth
b. 1903
d. 1903

years. After Isiah passed away, Sarah Murphy often called on him when she needed help with something.

For the next two hours, neighbors continued to pour into the parlor.

Family and friends remained at the Murphy homestead throughout the evening. In the tradition of the Irish wake, they toasted the deceased with a spread of food and spirits supplied by the Murphy clan. Tears turned to reverent chuckling as those who knew Gertrude shared humorous anecdotes. The last revelers said their farewells just before midnight.

The next day, the mourners gathered at the Springfield Cemetery, where Gertrude and Ruth Murphy were buried together in a family plot that already included Isiah, Sarah and William Murphy.

The ground over the new graves would still be loose when the gravediggers returned. Just ten days later, the Murphy curse would claim yet another victim whose death would lead to one of the most notorious criminal cases in the area's history.

Springfield Township, circa 1905, one mile north of the Murphy farm on State Road. The Springfield United Brethren Church and Clark School are north of the cemetery, and the Springfield Church of Christ and buggy shed are to the east. *Fife Lake Historical Society*.

Headstone of Gertrude Murphy at Springfield Township's Clark Cemetery. Gertrude was buried with her daughter, Ruth, who died the same day—April 20, 1903. *Photograph by Lisa Leach.*

In the weeks to come, several of the mourners would become caught in a web of suspicion, innuendo and allegation. Joe Battenfield would become a key witness in a murder investigation. A skeleton in Dan Murphy's closet would cause his neighbors to suspect him of foul play. Cousin Mary Mullen would spend a few hours behind bars for a crime she didn't commit. Margaret Chalker would publicly stand by one of her sisters although whispers of alleged wrongdoing would shake her faith to the core.

And standing at the center of the web would be a shadowy figure in a black taffeta dress, a woman who would become known as Michigan's Lucrezia Borgia.

"It's No Good, Joe, I Am Dying"

THE MURPHY FARM, SPRINGFIELD TOWNSHIP

Saturday, May 2, 1903

"Hold me down!"

Joe Battenfield heard the shrill cry from the upstairs bedroom as soon as he entered the Murphy house. He raced up the stairs of the small two-story farmhouse, taking the steps two at a time. Sarah Murphy hobbled up the stairs behind him to the same bedroom where, less than two weeks earlier, John's wife, Gertrude, had died.

Battenfield knew the Murphy family well. Sometimes when he ventured into nearby Fife Lake for supplies, he would pick up things for Sarah Murphy or her widowed daughter, Mary McKnight. Just four days earlier, on April 29, Mary had asked him to pick up the mail, to call on Dr. Pearsall to request a house call and to purchase five cents of strychnine—she wanted to kill some field mice that had gotten into the cellar. Battenfield dutifully bought the poison at LaBar's Drugstore and gave it to Mary Mullen when he passed by on his return trip.

If the Murphys needed something, it was usually John or Mary who did the asking. Their father, Isiah, passed away in 1894, leaving the farm in the hands of his widow, Sarah. In April, she celebrated her sixty-sixth birthday, but years of carving out a life in the north woods and raising nine children

Street view of downtown Fife Lake, circa 1910, by photographer Edward Beebe. The Hotel Gregory is on the left and the Brick Block to the right contained the Fife Lake Hardware, LaBar's Drugstore and W.W. Brower's General Store and Mortuary. *Fife Lake Historical Society.*

had taken their toll. She didn't get around as well as she used to and relied more and more on her children for the day-to-day business of the farm.

At about 9:00 p.m., Sarah Murphy appeared on Battenfield's doorstep. She was frantic and winded. Despite temperatures in the forties, beads of sweat covered her forehead. In between gasps for breath, she managed to explain. John had experienced sudden convulsions and crippling pain that left him prostrate in bed—the same strange symptoms Gertrude had experienced just before she died. Sarah feared John was to be the next victim of this awful curse that seemed to plague the Murphy clan, so she made a beeline for Battenfield's. She begged Joe to come at once and bring along a bottle of camphor.[8]

Inside the bedroom, Joe found a disturbing sight: John Murphy lying across the bed with his back arched so severely that his weight rested on the crown of his head. His hands were drawn up as if he was reaching in his vest pockets for something, and his legs were stretched straight out with his feet on the floor. His face was distorted, his lips were pulled back in a forced grin and his eyes were wide open. It looked like every muscle in his body was flexed. John's older sister Mary stood by the side of the bed, holding his hand.

"Joe," John managed to utter when he noticed his longtime friend enter the room. Battenfield reached into his pocket for the bottle of camphor and asked Mary to give John some salt. Mary fished a salt tablet out of a dish at the foot of the bed and placed it in John's hand. For a few seconds, John appeared to relax. His back flattened and his hands dropped to his sides.

Joe pulled the cork from the bottle and placed it in front of John's nose. "It's no good, Joe," John groaned. "I am dying."

"It cannot be that you are dying, John," Battenfield responded in disbelief.

"Yes, I am gone," John muttered.

Then, with a suddenness that startled Joe Battenfield, John's body convulsed in a violent spasm. His back arched, pulling his hands up to his chest and forcing his bodyweight back onto his head.

"Hold me down!" John screamed in agony. "My feet will come right up." In an attempt to pin down John's legs, Joe braced his right knee against John's.

The convulsion lasted for a few terrifying seconds. "It was just a minute. Almost like a moment, a few moments at least. His face was relaxed and he was gone," Battenfield later recalled.[9] He couldn't believe how fast it all happened. He had been there for only three to five minutes before John died.

When Mary realized John was gone, she began to sob.

Later that night, Joe helped Mary prepare John's body for the funeral. After Mary bathed her baby brother's body, she and Joe dressed John in his Sunday's best.[10] It was a real struggle; oddly, John's body remained stiff as a board.

Dr. Pearsall viewed the body a few hours later. John's arms and legs, Pearsall noticed, were still rigid. Typically, the limbs would become soft before rigor mortis caused them to stiffen, usually four or more hours after death unless some other factor changed the process. Several family members told Pearsall that John suffered from a long-term problem with asthma. During particularly troubling spells, they said, John clawed at the air as he gasped for breath. A severe asthma attack could, Pearsall knew, in some cases lead to a seizure.

He also knew that a violent death involving such a convulsion could lead to the rapid onset of rigor mortis. Just two weeks earlier, Gertrude Murphy had died after suffering from an identical wave of seizures, and he had noticed this same rigidity in her limbs. But the two deaths were too similar to be explained away as mere coincidence. Pearsall left the bedroom with a sense that he was once again missing something.

Somewhat baffled by the symptoms, Dr. S.E. Neihardt listed John's cause of death as shock following an asthma attack.[11] He decided not to

The interior of Brower's store, Fife Lake, circa 1900. *Fife Lake Historical Society.*

The undertaker's bill. Willis Brower sent this bill to Daniel C. Hutchins, the custodian of John Murphy's estate and the guardian of Gladys Murphy. Hutchins would later become involved in a battle over John Murphy's forty acres. *Collection of Lisa Leach.*

conduct a postmortem but wondered about the presence of a contagious and potentially fatal disease.

John Murphy was buried three days later at the Springfield Cemetery alongside his beloved Gertrude and Ruth. Joe Battenfield missed the funeral. Terrified by the possibility of a contagious and lethal disease plaguing the Murphy family, Dr. Neihardt placed Joe in quarantine.[12]

3

All in the Family

People in and around Springfield Township began to wonder about the curse hanging over the Murphy family, and they immediately suspected John's sister, Mary McKnight.

Mary had cared for all three Murphys just before they became ill. Gertrude left Ruth in Mary's care, and a neighbor saw Mary give the infant a tablet. Minutes later, the child suffered from a spasm. When John went to purchase a coffin, Gertrude remained behind with Mary, who gave her some medicine to calm her nerves.[13] Minutes later, Gertrude suffered from the first in a series of violent convulsions that led to her death. Mary also stood by John's side when he experienced a wave of seizures that left him bedridden with agonizing pain. She was still there, by her brother's bedside, when Joe Battenfield walked into the bedroom.

To folks around Springfield Township, Mary McKnight appeared more like an Angel of Death than a nurse. A few of the more religious residents thought of the Tenth Plague in the Book of Exodus and wondered what plague had afflicted John Murphy's family.

By mid-May, whispers about the mysterious Murphy deaths reached the ear of Kalkaska prosecutor Ernest C. Smith.

When in need of legal help, residents of Kalkaska turned to one of two men: Joshua L. Boyd or Ernest C. Smith.[14] Compared to Boyd, a twenty-five-year veteran of the law and Smith's predecessor as county prosecutor, twenty-nine-year-old Smith was a relative newcomer in the field of jurisprudence. A native of Kalkaska, Smith began practicing law in 1899, and after a few years in private practice, he won the position of prosecuting attorney. By May 1903, Smith had not yet argued a career-making case that would allow him to step out of Boyd's shadow, but that would all change in the coming months.

Shortly after the burial of John Murphy, Dr. Perly W. Pearsall stopped by Smith's office to discuss his concerns. Pearsall wasn't present when any of the Murphys died, but he saw the bodies immediately afterward. In each case, he noticed a peculiar rigidity in the muscles that baffled him. At first, Pearsall thought that John Murphy died from tetanus, but he dismissed it as a possibility because the onset of symptoms occurred much too rapidly for a tetanus case. Then, Pearsall wondered if John Murphy, like his wife, died following an epileptic seizure.

His suspicion piqued, Pearsall spoke with Joe Battenfield, who described in detail how John Murphy's body jackknifed backward during the last convulsion before he died. According to Battenfield, Murphy was quite aware during the convulsions, which wasn't consistent with an epileptic seizure. Battenfield also said John Murphy's face had become distorted during the convulsion episode—a grotesque grin that sent chills down his spine. Pearsall had pored through medical texts and found one scenario that appeared to fit all these symptoms: strychnine poisoning.

Joe Battenfield also told Pearsall that just a few days before John Murphy died, Mary McKnight had asked him to purchase five cents' worth of strychnine from a Fife Lake merchant. She wanted to kill some rats, she said, although none of the Murphys had seen any rodents around the place.

Smith sat forward in his chair.

The particulars of John Murphy's final moments seemed eerily familiar. He remembered reading in law school about a sordid case of strychnine poisoning that took place in Boston in 1860.

George Hersey fed his pregnant fiancée a spoonful of jam laced with strychnine in an apparent effort to abort the unwanted pregnancy. The sweet jam masked the bitter flavor of the poison, so Betsy Frances Tirrell didn't notice anything odd when she downed the concoction. That night, she suffered from a series of painful convulsions that caused her back to arch like a wishbone. During the violent spasms, her eyes widened, her

The document that led to one of the most infamous criminal cases in the history of northern Michigan. A clerk became suspicious when this mortgage document, detailing a loan from Mary McKnight to John Murphy, was brought into the county office for recording on May 7, 1903, just five days after John Murphy's death. The amount of the loan had been raised from $200 to $600. *Kalkaska County Register of Deeds.*

Kalkaska, circa 1900. One of most infamous murder cases in county history began when a clerk brought a peculiar mortgage document to the attention of prosecuting attorney Ernest C. Smith. *Author's collection.*

face contorted and she bit through her lip, leaving her face smeared with blood. After writhing in pain for several minutes, she died of what the family believed to be food poisoning.

Hersey tried to block the postmortem, saying that he didn't want his beloved's body damaged, but the family insisted. The postmortem revealed that Betsy, who was three months pregnant, died from a massive overdose of strychnine.

All eyes turned to Hersey. Authorities had learned that two other women associated with Hersey—a wife and a girlfriend—perished unexpectedly,

raising questions about the cause of death. His wife reportedly suffered from crippling convulsions on her deathbed, and an exhumation of his girlfriend's remains revealed the presence of strychnine.

A sweep of Betsy's room uncovered the murder weapon—a spoon—in the fireplace. It contained residue of strychnine. Hersey apparently had attempted to destroy the evidence of his crime.

During the trial, George Hersey maintained his innocence, claiming that Betsy had committed suicide, but the jury didn't buy his explanation. He was found guilty and sentenced to death. On the eve of his execution, Hersey confessed to murdering Betsy Frances but insisted he had nothing to do with the other two deaths.

Smith pondered the possibility that Mary McKnight was a female George Hersey, but the lack of any apparent motive troubled the young prosecutor. Then Smith heard a knock on his office door that would change everything.

Smith answered the door to find the register of deeds. Just a few days after John Murphy died, Mary McKnight brought in for recording a paper documenting changes to the mortgage on John Murphy's forty-acre farm.[15] The document was crisscrossed with erasures and alterations, but one change in particular caught the clerk's eye: the mortgage on the land had been raised from the initial amount of $200, which was crossed out and replaced with the figure of $600.

The prosecutor paid a visit to Alfred Kellogg, the justice of the peace. Kellogg remembered when John and Mary had brought the original mortgage to him. He eyeballed the document and identified the handwriting of both parties. The alteration, he believed, had been done by Mary McKnight's hand. The altered deed suggested a sinister, Machiavellian possibility: Mary first poisoned John's heirs—Gertrude and Ruth—and then poisoned John to obtain his forty acres of land.

On May 19, Smith made the first of three visits to the Murphy farm to question Mary McKnight about the mortgage document and the last days of John Murphy's life. He asked Sheriff Creighton to make the trip with him.

Shaking hands with forty-year-old Sheriff John W. Creighton was like squeezing a hand in a vice covered with sackcloth. His oversized, calloused hands were the products of decades spent wielding an axe.

Creighton grew up in the rugged frontier that was northern Michigan in the 1870s. Born in Canada on February 28, 1863, he crossed the border with his parents, Robert and Jane, just after the end of the Civil War. As a skilled blacksmith, Robert Creighton went to work in the lumber industry, helping others to clear the vast deciduous forests that blanketed the region. He acquired a homestead just a few miles from present-day Fife Lake, and the family became pioneers in the early settlement of the area. Young John worked from first light to sunset helping his father clear timber from the family spread.

In 1884, John wed Lavircia Richards, and the young couple worked the Creighton family farm until John won election as county sheriff in 1900. In the spring of 1903, he was midway through his second term.[16]

Smith and Creighton listened intently as Mary described John's death. Mary said she believed John had experienced an asthma attack. He could not catch his breath and smothered to death.[17]

When Smith asked about the mortgage, Mary explained the alteration. John took out a $200 mortgage on the property in 1899, she said, to raise the funds needed to build a new home. John wanted to increase the mortgage to $600 for cash he needed to make improvements, such as excavating a well. Mary McKnight lent him the money, and the mortgage was subsequently altered. But she just hadn't had the time to visit the register of deeds in Kalkaska so the change could be officially documented.[18]

Mary McKnight had offered an innocent and logical explanation for the alteration of the deed, but it was evident to Smith that John Murphy's death didn't result from an asthma attack. Dr. Pearsall's description of strychnine poisoning, coupled with Battenfield's recollection of John's final moments, left little doubt that Murphy had ingested an overdose of the deadly substance. Perhaps, Smith reasoned, the grief-stricken farmer could not cope with the loss of wife and child and committed suicide.

Lingering doubts caused Smith and Creighton to make a second trip to the Murphy farm a week later, on May 26. When the prosecutor mentioned his suicide theory, Mary was incredulous. There was no way, she said, that her brother committed suicide.

Smith then asked if there was any strychnine in the house that John could have used if he wanted to kill himself. The only poison at the Murphy homestead, Mary claimed, was in the cellar mixed with cornmeal and placed for the rats the previous winter.[19]

Smith and Creighton left the Murphy homestead with an uneasy feeling. There was something suspicious about the entire affair, so Smith started asking around. Back in Kalkaska, he learned that John had purchased a life insurance policy in the amount of $1,000. Since his wife and daughter preceded him in death, the money would go to his next of kin, his mother, Sarah. But with Sarah crippled by a lifetime of heavy labor, everyone knew that Mary McKnight was the de facto head of the family and would eventually gain control of the insurance money. Mary McKnight, Smith also learned, had made inquiries about the insurance policy shortly after her brother's death.

Mary's alleged plan to acquire control over her brother's life insurance inadvertently exposed a skeleton in the Murphy closet when an unexpected claimant stepped forward to dispute John's next of kin.

John had been married once before. In 1895, he wed sixteen-year-old Clara Gauld. But after just three months of marriage, he divorced her when he apparently came to believe that she had had an affair with his younger brother Dan.[20] Seven months after the divorce—on October 16, 1895—Gladys Murphy was born.[21] John denied paternity, but when Mary McKnight made overtures about collecting her brother's life insurance, the carrier disputed her claim on the grounds that it should go to his rightful heir, Gladys.

The altered mortgage and the life insurance, Smith believed, presented a powerful motive for murder, but so far, all the evidence was circumstantial, fueled by rumor and hearsay. To make a case, the prosecutor needed something more concrete, and he knew just where to look: six feet below John Murphy's headstone in the Springfield Cemetery.

"Don't You Ever Let Them Dig Me Up"

SPRINGFIELD CEMETERY, SPRINGFIELD TOWNSHIP, MICHIGAN

Friday, May 29, 1903[22]

The wind whipped across the Springfield Cemetery as Smith, Creighton and Dr. Pearsall stood by the grave of John Murphy and watched as two local men hoisted the coffin to ground level. The exhumation began at daybreak and took most of the morning.

Smith wanted Dr. Pearsall to remove John Murphy's stomach and send it to the University of Michigan to determine if he ingested strychnine before he died. As Pearsall watched the digging crew toss shovels of dirt from the grave, he thought back to his days in medical school.

While a student at Chicago's Homeopathical Medical College, Pearsall had an instructor who wanted to demonstrate the particular symptoms of strychnine poisoning. It was an important lesson for would-be doctors; several patent medicines contained small amounts of the drug. Taken in large amounts, however, it triggered a sequence of very distinct symptoms. Pearsall and the other students watched, wide-eyed, as the instructor pried open the jaws of a Newfoundland, inserted several tablets and massaged the canine's throat.

Within minutes, the dog began to show the first symptoms. As the poison affected the dog's central nervous system, it struggled to breathe and suffered

Springfield Township's Clark Cemetery and the Springfield Church of Christ and buggy shed in the background. On a frigid day in May, Sheriff Creighton, Prosecutor Ernest C. Smith and sextant John Jors exhumed the body of John Murphy. *Fife Lake Historical Society.*

Headstone of John Murphy at Springfield Township's Clark Cemetery. *Photograph by Lisa Leach.*

from the first in a series of convulsions. It dropped to the floor, its legs locked straight, its lips pulled back, its body twitching. Twenty minutes later, the movements stopped. That was the longest twenty minutes in Pearsall's college career.

In the fifteen years that had passed since his college days ended, Pearsall had set broken bones across the state of Michigan. He worked as a sawbones in Grand Ledge, Muskegon and Grand Rapids before settling in Kalkaska, where he had ministered to lumberjacks and farmers since 1895.[23] He amputated gangrenous limbs and pulled rotten teeth. He confronted typhoid and diphtheria, but his only experience with strychnine poisoning remained in that medical class.

Although he had never treated a patient suffering from strychnine poisoning, Pearsall knew something about the drug. Derived from the seeds of the *Strychnos nux-vomica* tree and other plants in the *Strychnos* genus, strychnine was often prescribed in small doses as a stimulant. It was a key ingredient in patent medicines such as Tincture of Nux Vomica and Easton's Syrup.

He also knew that in larger doses, strychnine was fatal—a fact quickly recognized by murderers. The white powder had a bitter taste that a would-be killer typically masked with another substance to avoid raising the suspicion of the intended victim. Often, it was dissolved in soup, tea, coffee or jam.

Pearsall thought about the dog. Human victims struggled through the same gut-wrenching agony as canines. The onset of symptoms—convulsions and difficulty breathing—took place within hours or even minutes of ingesting the drug. During this series of painful convulsions, the victim's muscles flexed and the back arched so severely that the body formed a bridge supported by the back of the head and the heels. Death occurred from exhaustion or respiratory failure, and the muscles remained rigid, often flexed, postmortem.

John Jors wedged a crowbar under the coffin lid. The pine creaked and snapped as the nails popped loose. He took a deep breath, reminded himself to breathe through his mouth and pushed the lid away. The sweet, pungent odor of rotting flesh overwhelmed Jors; he turned away and began to wretch. Smith and Creighton held handkerchiefs over their noses as Dr. Pearsall knelt down and examined the corpse.

Just as Pearsall suspected, the body presented outward signs of strychnine poisoning. "The feet were drawn," Pearsall later recalled, "and instead of lying flat as they usually do in a dead body they were drawn. Both hands were somewhat drawn across the breast."[24]

Pearsall removed a scalpel from his bag and went to work removing the stomach, lungs and liver. He placed the organs into two jars that Smith would send to Ann Arbor, where toxicology expert Dr. Ernest D. Reed would examine them.

Smith, though, decided not to wait for Reed's report. He ordered Creighton to arrest Mary McKnight and bring her to Kalkaska for questioning.

Creighton traveled to the Murphy homestead, but Sarah Murphy said that McKnight had left for Traverse City a few days earlier to obtain the help of an attorney. She wanted to prevent an exhumation of her brother. John, Mary later told Smith, gave her a deathbed commandment: "Don't you ever let them dig me up."

On the morning of May 31, Creighton finally caught up with Mary McKnight at Walton Junction. It was the logical place to look. The junction, southwest of Fife Lake in southern Grand Traverse County, was a major connecting point for the Grand Rapids and Indiana Railroad. Passengers traveling via train from Traverse City to Fife Lake passed through Walton Junction.

Creighton dreaded it whenever he had to go through the place. Considered one of the wildest spots in northern Michigan, lumberjacks crowded into the town on weekends, where they spent their hard-earned

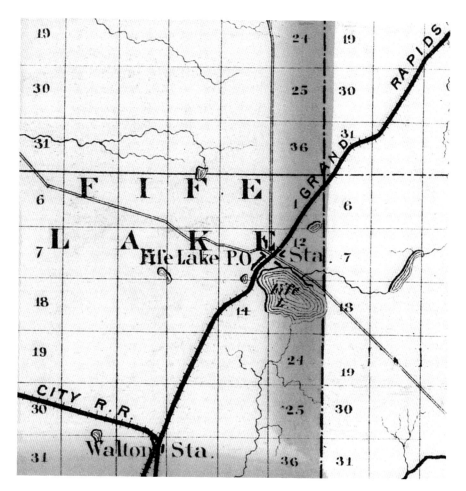

Close-up of Fife Lake from the Grand Traverse County map of the *H.F. Walling Atlas*. Walton Junction, southwest of Fife Lake, was one of the wildest spots in the Lower Peninsula and a key connection point on the GR&I Railroad line. Passengers traveling from Traverse City to Fife Lake would have switched trains here. On Sunday, May 31, Mary McKnight and her traveling companion, Mary Mullen, were arrested at Walton Junction. *Author's collection.*

coin on whiskey and women. The town hosted several saloons and bordellos that were choked with single men on Fridays and Saturdays. And the lumberjacks, who had their own form of justice, didn't like seeing a star walking around, but it was Sunday morning, so most of them would be in bed regretting that last shot from the night before.

The sheriff found Mary McKnight and her traveling companion, Mary Mullen, at the GR&I depot. The sheriff clamped bracelets on the two women and brought them back to Kalkaska for questioning.

View from Brower's Mortuary window looking west. This photograph was taken about 1910 by Beebe, a postcard photographer from Kalkaska. *Author's collection.*

Creighton interrogated Mary Mullen first. Battenfield said that he handed the five cents of strychnine to Mullen when he passed by the Murphy house on the way home from Fife Lake. Frightened, Mullen explained that she left the package on the kitchen table. When she looked at the table later, it was gone. She didn't know where it went.

It was clear to the sheriff that Mary Mullen was innocent of any wrongdoing, so he released her.

Mary McKnight wasn't as lucky. Creighton escorted her to the second story of the jail and locked her into the birdcage.

Meanwhile, Smith, carrying a large leather satchel, hopped a southbound train. One by one, other passengers nearby stood up and moved down the aisle as they caught a whiff of a peculiar odor emanating from Smith's valise. The prosecutor, though, didn't notice them. He was lost in his thoughts, as he wondered what secrets Dr. Reed would discover in John Murphy's stomach.

That afternoon, Dan Murphy traveled to Traverse City, where he asked attorney Parmius C. Gilbert and former Kalkaska prosecutor Joshua Boyd to take on his sister's case. The two lawyers made the perfect team. Gilbert was a tenacious litigator with a knack for prying the truth from stubborn witnesses, and Boyd was a twenty-five-year veteran of the law.

Born on May 5, 1856, Joshua L. Boyd grew up in Hillsdale, where his father—a carpenter who emigrated from County Tyrone, Ireland—ran a successful building firm. While his father helped build Hillsdale, Joshua studied law under a local attorney named Captain G.A. Knickerbocker. In 1878, he migrated north to Kalkaska, where he hung his shingle, defending inebriated lumberjacks and railroad men who crossed the law. He also began a long-running partnership with transplanted New Yorker William D. Totten.

In November of that same year, Boyd married Lulu E. Totten, his law partner's younger sister. Their first child died in infancy, but a few years later, Lulu gave birth to Lynn, who would later follow in his father's footsteps and enter the legal profession. Lulu Totten Boyd died in 1883.

Ill health forced Boyd to leave Michigan for the warmer, gentler climate of Kansas in 1886. After a two-year respite, he returned to Kalkaska, where he resumed his private practice until he became the county's prosecuting attorney around the turn of the century. By the spring of 1903, the forty-seven-year-old had amassed a trove of experience on both sides of the aisle, having defended the only two murder cases in the county's history. Now, he prepared to defend the accused in the most infamous murder case in the history of northern Michigan.[25]

Boyd and Gilbert hopped on the next train to Kalkaska, arriving at the jail at about the same time the sun dropped below the timberline. Sheriff Creighton met them at the door. With arms folded across his chest, he explained that on Smith's orders, no one could visit Mary McKnight.

Parm Gilbert was furious.

As they left the jail, they could see her silhouette sitting by the window.

Part 2

Rumor Has It

5
The Birdcage

KALKASKA JAIL

Monday, June 1, 1903

Ernest Smith returned from Ann Arbor on Monday evening and headed straight to the jail, where he hoped to pry a confession from Mary McKnight. His co-counsel was waiting. For help with the McKnight case, Smith had asked his mentor—former Kalkaska prosecuting attorney William D. Totten—to sit second chair.

The gnarly case became even more tangled when Totten agreed to join Smith. He had worked alongside Mary's defense attorney Joshua Boyd in private practice for twenty years before they dissolved their partnership in 1901. They had also married each other's sisters.

Totten grew up in New York but moved to northern Michigan as a teenager alongside his brother, Fred, and sisters Lulu, Adella and Nellie. In 1878, Lulu fell head-over-heels for Joshua Boyd. A year after the couple walked down the aisle, Totten was admitted to the state bar and went into business with his brother-in-law.

During one eventful Sunday dinner at the Boyd residence, Totten caught the eye of his partner's sister Ida, and in 1881, the couple tied the knot. The young bride gave birth to a daughter, Florence, but tragically, Ida Boyd Totten died in 1884. In 1885, Totten's sister Adella married local doctor Perly W. Pearsall.

Totten, like his young colleague Smith, knew criminal law from experience; he had served two terms as prosecuting attorney for the county of Kalkaska, from 1886 to 1890. In 1900, he won a spot in the Michigan state legislature, serving one term.[26]

Smith had just begun to brief his partner when he heard a commotion outside. The two men raced out of the office to the foot of the staircase leading to the second-story cells, where Sheriff Creighton stood toe to toe with Joshua Boyd.

Denied access to their client the night before, Boyd and Gilbert decided to try again, this time bringing Dan Murphy along. Once again, Creighton told them they could not go upstairs.

Boyd's face turned crimson when he noticed Totten approaching. Gilbert and Murphy watched the spectacle unfold as Boyd turned to Totten and demanded to see his client. The confrontation erupted into a shouting match. Boyd jabbed his finger at Totten's chest and accused him of unethical conduct. The back and forth continued for a few seconds before Parm Gilbert stepped in. Once again, the lawyers left without talking to their client.[27]

As Mary's legal team retreated, Smith went up to see his prisoner.

Mary rubbed her hands together as she answered Smith's questions. She repeated the same story she had told the prosecutor earlier. The only poison at the Murphy house was in the cellar. The previous winter, she had mixed strychnine with cornmeal and placed the cakes in the cellar to kill the mice. She did not, she said, have any strychnine of her own, and she did not purchase any, either.

Smith reminded Mary about what he called the "Battenfield poison"—five cents' worth of strychnine Joe Battenfield purchased, at Mary's request, from LaBar's Drugstore in Fife Lake.

Mary looked around the room as if searching for an answer. She had forgotten about it at first, she said. That was the poison that she mixed in the cornmeal and placed in the cellar, but, she said, she erred in the date. She mixed the poison with the cornmeal a few days—not a few months—before John's death.

There were, Mary added, some "antiseptic tablets" in the house that probably did contain small amounts of strychnine. But she insisted she did not give John any medicine the night he died. And she was sure that he didn't take any either.

Smith just shook his head as he looked at the suspect. Mary managed to weave the "Battenfield poison" into a convenient story that provided an innocent explanation for why she purchased strychnine on the eve of her brother's death.

By Wednesday, June 3, Mary McKnight had become a physical wreck. She stopped eating and began to lose weight at an alarming rate. Creighton, worried about his prisoner's health, told Smith that "she was in a very much disturbed condition mentally." So the prosecutor decided to check on Mary.

That afternoon, Smith visited the jail. Mary was sitting on the cot in her cell when the prosecutor arrived. "I found her in a very nervous condition and in a condition which very much excited my sympathy toward her," he later recalled. "I thought at that time that there must be some relief for the woman or else she could very soon lose her reason."

"Mrs. McKnight," Smith said in a soft, reassuring voice, "I have not come to talk about the case in any way, and I do not wish you to talk about it. I simply came to see how you were getting along."

Mary looked at him with a blank expression.

Smith continued, "I presume you think because I am the prosecuting attorney, that I am necessarily an enemy of yours. Your condition excites my sympathy, and although I am the prosecuting attorney, if I can do anything to alleviate your sufferings I shall be glad to do it. If there is anything you want me to do, if there is any way in which I can help you, let me know, and if I can do it, I will do so. Have you ever been affiliated with any church?"

Mary hesitated for a moment. She said she once belonged to the Baptist Church and asked if there was one in town.

Smith nodded and said he thought Mary would like to meet the Baptist clergyman. Mary agreed and asked the prosecutor to bring him to the jail for a visit.

"I know you cannot be my attorney," Mary said, "but is there any reason why you cannot be a friend to me?"

"No, Mrs. McKnight, if I can do anything to alleviate your suffering, your present physical condition, I shall be glad to do so, but I want to have a fair and square understanding with you at this time. Mrs. McKnight, I have canvassed the situation from every stand point and have looked up the evidence from every stand point, and I cannot arrive at any conclusions possible, except that you administered the poison to John Murphy. If there was any possible doubt in my mind I would gladly give it to you, but I want to have a perfect and fair understanding with you right at this time upon that question. I have not come to talk with you about this case. You know what I believe about it, and I cannot believe anything different."

Mary just stared at him in silence. As Smith stood up from the chair and started to the door, she said, "Well, I am glad you have come and I feel better. Will you come tomorrow and bring the clergyman?"[28] Smith agreed to visit the jail the next day with the minister.

That evening, Smith received word from Ann Arbor. Dr. Reed had concluded his study of John Murphy's internal organs. The victim's stomach contained five-sixths of a grain of strychnine, which indicated that he had swallowed an even larger dose since some of the poison had been absorbed into his bloodstream before he died. The typical medicinal dose found in patent medicines such as Easton's Syrup ranged from between one-thirtieth and one-sixtieth of a grain. John Murphy had downed enough poison to kill a dozen men.

There was no longer any doubt: someone had poisoned John Murphy, and she wasn't ready to confess her sins. Smith realized that he needed leverage to pry the truth from Mary McKnight, and he knew just where he could find it.

The next morning, Smith, Creighton, Dr. Pearsall and a digging crew returned to Springfield Cemetery to exhume the bodies of Ruth and Gertrude Murphy. With a few deft swipes of his scalpel, Pearsall managed to remove the stomachs, which he placed in jars.

A few hours later, Smith was once again on a train bound for Dr. Reed's laboratory in Ann Arbor. After depositing the jars, he spent the rest of the weekend investigating Mary McKnight's background. He spoke with friends, relatives and neighbors and uncovered a shocking trail of suspicious deaths.

"Prosecutor Smith is a young and able attorney," a writer for the *(Traverse City) Evening Record* gloated, "and is leaving no stone unturned to sift this mystery to the bottom."[29]

6
Skeletons in Her Closet

KALKASKA, MICHIGAN

Sunday, June 7, 1903

Mary McKnight owned a fancy black dress that she wore to funerals, and throughout her adult life, Smith discovered, she had plenty of opportunities to wear it.

The prosecutor stared at a sheet of paper on his desk containing a list of names and dates. The entries began with "John Murphy, May 2, 1903" and went in reverse chronological order. Next came Gertrude Murphy, April 20, 1903, followed by Ruth Murphy. Smith ran his finger down the entire list and counted twelve names. Everywhere Mary McKnight went, death appeared to follow.

The eldest daughter of Canadian immigrant Isiah Murphy and Sarah Timmons, Mary Murphy was born in Canada in 1857. At thirteen, she crossed the border with her parents and settled in Alpena County, where her father worked at a local sawmill until he purchased a tract of land in Kalkaska County.

As a young teenager, Mary left home and moved into the boardinghouse of William and Sophronia Leach in Alpena. While there, she worked as a domestic servant, doing the laundry for the other boarders who were employed at a local sawmill. Mary may also have acquired some knowledge about medicine and midwifery from Dr. Louis Serrghras, who also lived at the Leach boardinghouse.[30]

A lumberjack camp in northern Michigan, circa 1892. Isiah Murphy and his boys farmed their land in Springfield Township during the spring and summer months and worked in the lumberjack camps during the winter. Mary McKnight spent her early teenage years working at an Alpena boardinghouse where several lumberjacks lived. *Library of Congress.*

Considered an attractive girl, Mary caught the eye of James D. Ambrose, a local painter. On April 19, 1876, nineteen-year-old Mary wed Ambrose. Their marriage endured one tragedy after another. The couple lost three children in infancy. Eventually, they had two daughters, Minnie and May.

Tragedy again struck the Ambroses in the summer of 1882, when four-year-old Minnie went to visit her grandmother in Monroe. While there, she caught diphtheria. Mary was too ill to travel, so James raced south. By the time he reached Monroe, Minnie had died.

In 1884, Mary and her two-year-old daughter, May, traveled to Saginaw, where Mary wanted to visit some old friends. While on the train, they both became sick. They were immediately carted to a hospital, where Mary made a full recovery. Tragically, May Ambrose didn't. Like her sister before her, she died of diphtheria.

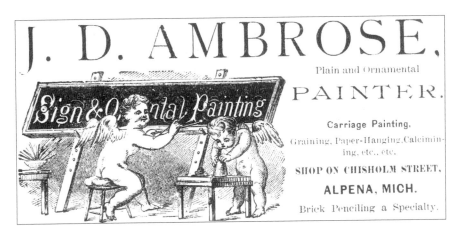

This advertisement for James Ambrose's painting business appeared in the 1883 Alpena city guide. *Author's collection.*

A few years later—in 1887—James Ambrose mysteriously fell ill and died.

Smith interviewed neighbors, who described James's death. According to eyewitnesses, he spent his last moments thrashing in agony, his limbs twitching in spasmodic convulsions. Mary collected $2,000 from her husband's life insurance policy.

Widowed, alone and away from home, Mary moved in with James's business partner, James Ernest McKnight, and his wife. In July 1887, McKnight's wife became seriously ill, suffering from a sudden onset of convulsions. Her sister, Gib Teeple, rushed to Alpena along with her husband and their baby daughter. Gib left her baby in Mary's care while she stayed at her sister's bedside, but no amount of nursing helped. Mrs. McKnight died the night the Teeples arrived. The next day, Baby Teeple also got sick. Neighbors said the baby suffered from convulsions before she, too, died.

Smith next traced Mary's movements to Saginaw, where she went to live with her sister Margaret Chalker. James McKnight, now a widower, had fallen for Mary, and the two planned to exchange vows. Mary spent the three-week interim with Margaret; her husband, William; and their three children.

After the wedding, Mary McKnight moved to Alpena with James. She remained close with her sister, periodically taking the southbound train to visit the Chalker family.

It was during one of these visits that her thirteen-year-old niece, Eliza Chalker, became sick following afternoon tea with Aunt Mary. Smith found eyewitnesses who said the girl suffered from convulsions. Her limbs jerked, and she foamed at the mouth before dying on May 3, 1892. Dr. Woodworth considered her death the result of congestive grip.

Smith discovered that a parallel incident occurred less than a year later during another one of Mary's visits to the Chalker residence. On February 18, 1893, Mary's eighteen-year-old sister, Sarah Murphy, traveled to Saginaw to visit her fiancé. While enjoying a cup of afternoon tea with Aunt Mary and Aunt Margaret, Sarah excitedly described her betrothed. The three women giggled and talked about wedding arrangements.

Suddenly, Sarah's body began to twitch and convulse. Terrified, the women called for Dr. Woodworth, who prescribed a mustard bath. Mary and Margaret tried to keep Sarah's body immersed, but the spasms caused her arms and legs to violently thrust out of the water. She died four and a half hours after the twitching began.

The next chapter of Mary's story took place in Grayling. In 1894, the McKnight couple moved to a farm that James purchased. For four years, Mary's life was unmarred by any mysterious deaths. That all changed one dark night in the fall of 1898.

On November 12, 1898, James McKnight became deathly ill after eating a dinner that Mary sent to him as he worked in the fields. The attending physician, Dr. Leighton, told Smith that when he arrived at the McKnight residence, James was on his deathbed.

Leighton detailed the symptoms. James McKnight's torso was bent backward like a bow, his arms and legs jerked and his throat became partially paralyzed.

But then, after two days of lying in bed, McKnight's condition began to improve. He sat up in bed, smoked a pipe and chuckled about his brush with death. Leighton believed McKnight would survive the ordeal, so he returned to town.

That same evening, McKnight relapsed and died. Mary told Leighton that her husband's relapse occurred so quickly that she didn't have time to call for help. Puzzled, Dr. Leighton listed the immediate cause of McKnight's death as exhaustion brought on by paralysis.[31] Now, after discussing the case with Smith, Leighton was convinced McKnight had died from strychnine poisoning. After the funeral, Mary collected another $2,000 from her second husband's life insurance policy.

Over the next few years, other mysterious deaths occurred around Mary McKnight.

In 1900, Mary received word that an old friend in Saginaw named Mrs. McKenzie died following a surgery, and her grandmother Mrs. Schneeburger had become sick with grief. Mary traveled east to care for the old lady's house, and while there, Mrs. Schneeburger suddenly died. A few days later, Mrs. Schneeburger's daughter, Mrs. Curry, also died. The timing was suspicious, but Smith failed to find any witnesses who could describe their symptoms.

Despite a cloud of death constantly hovering over Mary McKnight, her friends and neighbors continued to seek her help. When Anna Jenson became sick and had to go to the hospital in Grayling, she turned to Mary McKnight for help, leaving her six-year-old daughter, Dorothy, in Mary's care.

On March 28, 1902, Dorothy became sick after playing with her friends in the yard. Mary told a neighbor that the girl overdid it and was exhausted from skipping rope, but the neighborhood kids told Smith they noticed a strange trembling that seemed to shake Dorothy's entire body and that she frothed at the mouth like a rabid dog.

Dorothy Jenson was already dead when local physician Stanley Insley arrived about four o'clock in the afternoon. On the girl's death certificate, he stated that she "died suddenly after fainting" and estimated her death occurred in a period of minutes. As for cause of death, the baffled doctor wrote, "Don't know" and listed "over exertion, skipping rope" as a contributory factor.[32]

In the winter of 1903, Mary took up residence in her mother's home in Springfield Township. Within months, three more suspicious deaths rocked the Murphy household. That spring, her brother John; his wife, Gertrude; and their daughter, Ruth, all perished after suffering from the same symptoms as Dorothy Jenson and James McKnight.

Smith studied his handwritten list. He knew better than to draw conclusions based solely on interviews with friends and neighbors, but all the deaths shared similarities that were hard to dismiss as mere coincidence.

A portion of the death certificate showing cause of death for Dorothy Jenson, who died suddenly in March 1902. Mystified, the attending physician believed she might have died of overexertion after "skipping rope." As for her cause of death: "Don't know." *Michigan Department of Community Health.*

According to Dr. Pearsall, victims of strychnine poisoning died within a few hours after the onset of symptoms. Almost everyone on the death list had passed away only a brief time after becoming ill. Smith glanced at Dorothy Jenson's death certificate. According to Dr. Insley's notes, the girl died just minutes after fainting. Smith wondered if little Dorothy fainted after experiencing a convulsion.

Yet Smith realized that if Mary McKnight used poison to hack off several branches of her family tree, her motive remained unclear. She collected $4,000 in life insurance money after the deaths of her two husbands, but why kill the others? The absence of motive troubled the prosecutor. Wild theories were circulating throughout northern Michigan. Mary, some said, used poison to ease the anguish of those in her care, accidentally overdosing them in the process. But surely Mary, with all her nursing experience, knew how much strychnine was too much.

Besides, Dr. Reed discovered that John Murphy had ingested an amount of strychnine several times over the lethal amount. Perhaps Mary fed them an overdose on purpose, saving Gertrude from a life of pining over her lost child and John from pining over Gertrude. This would not, however, explain why she would have poisoned Ruth in the first place.

Other folks speculated about a darker motive. Mary, they argued, liked to attend funerals. An Irish wake was a major social event, and Mary enjoyed the morbid ceremonies so much that she found a way to create them.

Smith glanced at the list, and he felt his stomach tighten. Several children died while in Mary McKnight's care. Since Mary lost all five of her own children, perhaps these other deaths resulted from a twisted envy for the family she could never have.

The prosecutor set down the list. It was all baseless speculation. If, however, Dr. Reed found strychnine in the stomachs of Ruth and Gertrude Murphy, it would no longer be baseless.

Nosy news reporters didn't fail to notice the cloud of morbidity that surrounded Mary McKnight wherever she went. The *Detroit News Tribune* ran a front-page item entitled "Death in Her Train." The fact that "more than a dozen persons related to or intimately associated with her have died, has inspired the suspicion that she is after all a modern Borgia, and that the destruction of human life has become with her a mania."[33]

By calling McKnight a "modern Borgia," the *Tribune* writer linked Mary with Italy's Lucrezia Borgia—an infamous Renaissance debutante who allegedly poisoned several people. Michigan's Borgia had been christened.

Portrait of a woman, presumed to be the infamous Renaissance figure Lucrezia Borgia, by Italian artist Bartolomeo Veneto. Mary McKnight was frequently called the Michigan Borgia, a twisted homage to the infamous Renaissance debutante. According to legend, Lucrezia wore a hollow ring containing poison, but many historians believe her reputation as a poisoner was the result of baseless rumormongering by her enemies. *Wikipedia Commons.*

The *(Traverse City) Evening Record* ran a parallel page-one item that depicted the Michigan Borgia as more of a victim than a perpetrator of multiple murders: "Death has walked in her footsteps and torn from her many of her closest relatives and dearest friends. It would seem that the bestowal of her

Portrait of Mary McKnight, circa 1903. This photograph appeared in the June 10, 1903 edition of the *(Detroit) Evening News*. Some said Mary was quiet, indifferent and antisocial. Others said she was affable and gregarious. *Author's collection.*

love upon a human being was to be punished by the striking down of the object of her affection."

The *Evening Record* writer went on to aver that the myriad tragedies in Mary's life should make her an object of pity, but instead, "her very misfortunes are being used against her by those who know her best and from whom, therefore, one might expect the first words of solace for her."[34] This was a direct indictment of Mary's friends and family.

Sarah, Dan and Charles Murphy answered the reporter's not-so-subtle insinuation by stepping forward in a desperate attempt to clear Mary's name. They put forth an alternative theory: John Murphy poisoned his wife and child before taking his own life—a claim that appeared in the next day's edition of the *Evening Record*.

Incredulous, Sheriff Creighton responded, "That's all rot. It's not even a possibility in view of the evidence we have picked up in the past few days."[35]

With Mary a fixture on front pages across the state, friends and relatives came forward to proclaim her innocence. Mary's best friend, Mrs. Woolover, presented a letter to the *(Detroit) Evening News*, which published portions of it in its June 6, 1903 edition. Mary had penned the note in late April, just after the deaths of Ruth and Gertrude Murphy.

"My brother's wife came here with her baby, 8 months old," Mary wrote. "It took cold coming, and took sick and died. She was sick when the baby was, and after it died she went into convulsions, one after the other, until she died. So you can see what trouble we have been in. She was buried yesterday. I don't know what will come next. I am feeling awful bad and have a terrible cold."[36] In the note, Mary also spoke of a longtime affliction that she feared would cause her death.

Woolover told the *Evening News* reporter that she witnessed the deaths of both Mrs. McKnight and Mr. Ambrose. "I know what ailed the first Mrs. McKnight," she said, "and I know what killed her. And I know, too, that the present Mrs. McKnight had nothing to do with the death of several others, which are hinted at as due to her influence."[37]

Despite Mrs. Woolver's attempt to exonerate Mary, readers quickly jumped to their own conclusions. Mary McKnight, whose "longtime affliction" had led to a homicidal "mania," dosed her relatives with strychnine, which caused the multiple convulsions "one after the other."

Miss Vinn Curry, whose mother appeared on the Michigan Borgia's list of probable victims, inked a letter to Mary from her home in East Tawas. "We all believe you innocent. Papa wants to come to see you. If there is anything we can do for you let us know."[38]

Smith left little doubt about his convictions when, a few days after the Michigan Borgia became a news sensation, he made a public statement:

> *The case is not altogether circumstantial, although that style of evidence predominates. We have what I believe to be a very strong case. The evidence we have collected from the surviving members of her family and her own conflicting statements combine in one damning mass of evidence. As it stands now, I believe we have enough evidence to convict Mrs. McKnight of the murder of her own brother, his wife, an inoffensive girl of 29 years, and possibly of their baby of three months. We have discovered new evidence which greatly strengthened our case, but it is of such a nature that we cannot safely disclose it until after the arraignment of the defendant. No one else is under suspicion.*[39]

The prosecutor chose his words well. Aware of the public sentiment regarding Mary, he hinted at other alleged murders when he spoke about collecting evidence from "the surviving members of her family." Northern Michiganders read between the lines of Smith's statement: the "surviving" Murphys were lucky to be alive.

7

Confession

KALKASKA JAIL

Monday, June 8, 1903

A week had passed, and Mary still hadn't seen any of her friends and relatives. Her sister Martha Woodard dropped by the jail on June 5, but Creighton chased her away.

By the end of the week, Smith softened and let Joshua Boyd visit his client, although only in the presence of the sheriff. During several meetings over the weekend, Boyd tried to counsel Mary as Creighton hovered over them. Mary and her lawyer discussed the case until 9:30 p.m. on the evening of June 8.

As Creighton escorted Boyd out of the cell, Mary tugged at the sheriff's sleeve. Creighton leaned down, and she whispered into his ear. She wanted him to telephone Smith and ask him to come to the jail. She had to tell him something.

Smith arrived just as Boyd left the building. Mary sat forward when Smith walked into the room. He noticed that she was rubbing her hands together.

"Mrs. McKnight," Smith said, "I believe you are carrying an awful weight upon you and that you will enjoy probably no peace of mind or quiet until you relieve yourself from it." His voice was gentle and reassuring.

Mary's lips curled up at the edges as she attempted a smile.

"I do not wish you to tell me anything," Smith continued. "Of course, your attorneys have instructed you that you should not talk to me. I do not wish you to tell me anything regarding the case, but I do say to you that you will not find relief of your present mental condition until you unburden yourself to someone."

"I know I ought not to talk to you," Mary responded. "Mr. Boyd has told me every day he has been here under no circumstances to have anything to say to you." Mary hesitated. "I am going to talk anyway."

Smith listened without interrupting as Mary described the circumstances of John's and Gertrude Murphy's deaths. She admitted to giving them medicine but insisted that she never intended to harm either of them.

"I had this strychnine and some quinine mixed together in capsules. When Gertie's baby died, I thought it would soothe her if I gave her one of the capsules. I didn't mean to harm her. Then Gertrude died," Mary explained. "I did the same with John. I did not intend to hurt my own brother. I thought the capsule would soothe him. It seemed to kill him, though. I didn't give the baby anything. I don't know how it came to die."[40]

When Mary finished, Smith asked her what kind of medicine Ruth Murphy took.

She ignored the question. "Will you come over again tomorrow?" she asked. "I want to talk to you and I wish you could come over."

On the way to his office, Smith kept rehashing Mary's statement in his mind. Something was wrong with her explanation. One capsule with a medicinal dose of strychnine would not have been enough to kill either Gertrude or John Murphy. Besides, the amount of poison Dr. Reed found in John's stomach indicated the victim took over twenty times more than the typical medicinal dose and almost double the lethal dose of half a grain. And despite Mary's denial, Smith was convinced she also poisoned Ruth Murphy. He hoped Dr. Reed would find the proof he needed.

The next afternoon—June 9—Smith received word from Ann Arbor. Dr. Reed's telegram was short and to the point. Smith reread the telegram as he pulled on his jacket:

Strychnine in Baby Murphy's stomach and Mrs. Murphy.

Dr. E.D. Reed[41]

Smith handed Mary the telegram as he entered her cell. She slowly read the text and handed it back to the prosecutor. Once again, Mary began to grind her hands together. After a long pause, she began to talk.

This time, Mary admitted giving poison to all three, including the baby. She intended to give Ruth Murphy some anti febrim, she said, which she kept on the shelf next to her strychnine, but she tragically reached for the wrong package. As for Gertrude and John Murphy, Mary insisted she administered pills containing a medicinal amount of strychnine to comfort them and nothing more. The deaths were accidental, she said, not homicidal. Throughout her statement, Mary kept repeating, "I didn't intend to hurt any of them."

Yet this, Smith realized, was where Mary had drifted from reality to fantasy. The prisoner did occasionally take a concoction of strychnine and quinine, and by her own admission, she gave one pill to Gertrude and two or three to John Murphy. But if each capsule contained the medicinal dose of between one-thirtieth to one-sixtieth of a grain, then two to three would not explain the massive dose of strychnine—five-sixths of a grain—found in John Murphy's stomach.

Then again, it appeared that Mary made her own capsules, so perhaps her medicine for some reason contained more strychnine than the average medicinal dose.

Smith smirked and stared at Mary McKnight. He could believe she accidentally overdosed one but not all three. It was more likely she purposefully administered a fatal dose. Nonetheless, it was strychnine that had killed the three Murphys, and Mary had just admitted giving it to them. The suspect, Smith believed, had just confessed to a triple murder in a roundabout way. But there was no one else present to witness the shocking statement. Boyd and Gilbert would immediately denounce it as hearsay, or worse, accuse Smith of coercing a so-called confession.

Kalkaska County didn't have a professional stenographer, so Smith came up with a plan.

"Have you any objections to my putting this in writing and your signing it?" Smith asked after a lengthy pause. He promised to write the statement exactly as Mary made it.

Mary just stared at the prosecutor with a blank expression. Smith realized that if he wanted a signed statement, he would have to do some prodding.

"You say you have given this strychnine without intent to harm any of these people," Smith continued. "Do you want all the world to know how you claim that John and Gertrude and baby Murphy come to their death? Do you want your people to know that?"

"It is true," Mary nodded, "and I want them all to know."[42]

Over the next few minutes, Smith penned the statement. When finished, he read it aloud:

I didn't intend harm to any of them. I did give the baby the strychnine. It woke up and cried while its mother was gone, and I mixed up a little of the strychnine in a glass with some water and gave a spoonful of it to the baby. I didn't mean to harm the little thing at all. I confessed all I did, to the Lord, this afternoon, and I feel that he has forgiven me.

When Gertrude came home and found the baby dead, she got awfully nervous. She knew she was nervous and all worked up, and she came to me and said: "Mary, can't you give me something to quiet me? Something that you take yourself?" I said that I would, and I really didn't think that it would hurt her if I gave her one of the capsules. She had spasms right after that, and I suppose that it was the strychnine that killed her. I really didn't mean to hurt her, though. I loved Gertie. I was awfully sorry to see her go.

Then John seemed to feel so badly about it, so broken up, that I often thought, after Gertie died, that it would be for the best if he were to go too. I really didn't mean to hurt him, though. He comes and sees me now at nights, and so does Gertrude, and they talk to me. They tell me that they forgive me. The Lord has forgiven me, too.

John was feeling bad one night a couple of weeks after Gertie died, and he came to me and said he wanted something to quiet him. He was suffering from asthma, too. I had two or three of the capsules on my dresser, and I told him to go and get one of them. I had two or three capsules filled with strychnine and quinine in the cover of a pill box on my dresser, and he went up and helped himself. I don't know whether he took one or two.

Then he went to bed, and I went to bed, too, and by and by I heard him call, and I went to his room. He said that he was having a chill. Mother came, too. By and by he began to have those same spasms, and I suppose that the strychnine was working. I suppose that is really what killed him, though I didn't intend to hurt any of them.

I loved John. He was always a good brother to me. I loved Gertie, too. I was sorry to see John go, but I suppose it was all for the best. John has come to me, and Gertie, too, since I have been in jail, and they have told me that they forgive me. I told the Lord all about it, too, and I am sure that he has forgiven me.[43]

After reading the last paragraph, Smith handed the document to Mary, who briefly looked it over before scrawling her signature at the bottom of the page.

In the scripted confession, Smith had failed to mention Mary's explanation about the mix-up of drug packages in the death of Ruth Murphy. This omission would play a major role in the tone of the subsequent media coverage and the public's perception of Mary McKnight.

The middle-aged widow from Springfield Township was about to become a nationwide news sensation.

8

The Michigan Borgia

KALKASKA, MICHIGAN

Wednesday, June 10–Sunday, June 14, 1903

The lack of a viable motive was a head-scratcher, but Smith was convinced that he and Creighton had wrenched a true confession from their suspect. The next morning, Smith released a transcript of the confession and gave a public statement about Mary McKnight's admission:

> *Overburdened by the horrible crime with which she was suspected, Mrs. Mary McKnight sent for me Monday and Tuesday evenings and finally confessed voluntarily that she had administered poison to her brother, to his wife, and to the baby. Her arrest and confinement and the burden of her guilt had overcome even her strong will, until she felt that she could no longer withhold her terrible secret from the world. Mrs. McKnight admitted freely that she had administered strychnine to Baby Murphy, Gertrude Murphy, and John Murphy.*[44]

Even though Mary insisted the deaths were accidental, Smith's announcement reflected his belief about her intent. Mary's guilty conscience hounded her into relinquishing a "terrible secret," which was murder.

That evening—June 10—Smith, Creighton, Boyd and a *Detroit Free Press* reporter whom Smith had invited gathered in the office of Justice Kellogg for the arraignment. "It was a weird scene in the little office of the Justice where the formal arraignment took place in the dim twilight," wrote the *Free Press* reporter. "The officials conferred in a few words of subdued tones while the stifled sobs of the prisoner heard at intervals made it an occasion of considerable solemnity."

Mary left an impression on the only member of the press allowed to be an eyewitness to the arraignment: "While she has a strong, shrewd face, it does not impress one as being that of a woman capable of calmly plotting the death of several persons, and those people her own relatives."[45]

Over the next few days, newspapers across Michigan ran stories about the Michigan Borgia's confession. Some papers included verbatim portions of the alleged "confession"; others ran the entire statement. Although Mary never admitted to murder—a fact clear from her "confession"—reporters followed Smith's precedent and condemned her as a triple murderess anyway.

The *(Detroit) Evening News* June 10 edition contained a front-page item under a headline that left little doubt about Mary's guilty intent: "Mrs. M'Knight Makes a Full Confession: Overcome by Remorse and Sorrow, Kalkaska Woman Owns to Poisoning Her Brother, His Wife and Infant Daughter."

The *(Traverse City) Evening Record*'s June 11 headline story was even more direct in its indictment: "Mrs. McKnight Has Confessed to Triple Murder." The *Evening Record* journalist speculated about Mary's as-yet-uncertain motive. "It is now accepted here that Mrs. McKnight is the murderer of at least the three Murphys," the correspondent wrote, "but her motive still remains a mystery, unless she has a mania for slaughter. The mercenary motive does not seem strong enough, and the way in which it appeared that she hoped to benefit by the death of the Murphys seemed so uncertain that this is not considered the real motive."[46]

The *Detroit Tribune* sentenced Mary, six months before the trial took place, with the headline "SHE IS GUILTY." The writer errantly noted that her confession "shatters the faith held in her by every relative and near friend." In reality, Dan Murphy, Charlie Murphy and Margaret Chalker remained faithful advocates of Mary McKnight despite the onslaught of negative media coverage and the damning statement she signed.

The *Tribune* article vilified McKnight as "either a cold-blooded murderess or the victim of an uncontrollable homicidal mania" and provided a list of other potential victims.[47] The author also noted a strange duality in Mary's admissions; she said she loved her relatives and wanted to soothe their pain but gave them fatal doses of poison. "Expressing love for her victims, and in spite of the fatal effects of the medicine she gave them, repeating in apparent sincerity her purpose as only to alleviate pain, she now avers faith in their return to earth to forgive her."[48]

The *Alpena Evening News* ran an item under the headline "MODERN BORGIA." The article not only contained Mary's full confession but also repeated the list of "Probably Poisoned," beginning with Alpena native (and Mary's first husband) James Ambrose.[49]

Like the *Alpena Evening News*, the *Toledo Sunday Bee*'s page-one headline played on the nickname coined by a brother reporter a few days earlier in Detroit: "Modern Lucretia Borgia." The article's subtitle erroneously claimed that "Mrs. McKnight Confessed to Long List of Horrors." The *Bee* article went on to detail eight of the Borgia's other alleged victims.[50]

By Thursday, June 11, the ugly story of a sister who used poison to erase her brother's entire branch of the family tree drifted out of the Midwest, making headlines across the country. The *New York Times* ran an item about the crime under the headline "Woman Confesses to Killing Three Persons."

"Her confession to-day was entirely voluntary," the *Times* reporter said in concluding his article, "and she seemed perfectly sane, although under great mental strain. No motives for the crime can be found."[51]

The *Times* writer foresaw a growing controversy taking place in Kalkaska. Ernest C. Smith faced allegations that Mary's statement wasn't "entirely voluntary," and Sheriff John Creighton faced allegations of mistreating the prisoner.

A *(Detroit) Evening News* reporter managed to tiptoe past Creighton and up the stairs of the Kalkaska jail, remaining unnoticed just long enough to catch a glimpse of the mysterious Mary McKnight. The staff correspondent, who signed her articles under the name of "Janette," characterized Mary as "caged like an animal" and wrote a lengthy description of her confines: "A room 18 or 20 feet square on the upper floor of the two-story wooden building...such is the prison cell of the woman upon whom are fixed in horror the eyes of all of northern Michigan, perhaps of the whole state."[52]

Janette went on to describe Mary's birdcage: "In the center of the big room stands a structure which forces [a] smile into the mind of the observer at first glance. It is an iron cage. The bars of the cage reach to the ceiling. The floor is of boiler iron. The furnishings are an iron bed and bed clothing. The cage is just a little bigger than the bed."[53]

Then the intrepid reporter described the moment she came face-to-face with Mary McKnight: "The curious observer tiptoeing to the door has a vision of a medium-sized woman with black hair, dressed in a red waist and a skirt of dark material. At the sound of footsteps, her head is turned, and a pair of grey-black eyes flash a look of fear at the intruder."[54]

On Wednesday evening, Joshua Boyd climbed the stairs of the Kalkaska jail with a roll of folded newspapers under his arm. Boyd later described Mary McKnight's reaction to the news of her alleged confession: "Confess! Confess!" she shrieked. "Never, never, never. I did not kill them. I did not say so. It is a lie."[55]

"I had a long talk with her," Boyd told reporters after the meeting, "and went over the alleged confession in detail. She denied it in toto. She said in unmistakable terms that she had not confessed anything, and that she had nothing to confess. 'I am innocent of any wrong doing,' she said, 'I didn't make any statement at all.'"[56]

Boyd blasted Creighton and Smith by implying they had coerced the so-called confession. "I do not believe that my client has ever made any voluntary confession," Boyd told the press. "She protested her innocence in the most touching and impressive manner this morning."

Boyd chose his words carefully. With his next sentence, he hinted at a possible future defense strategy by raising the issue of Mary's sanity. "If such a statement was wrung from her after she had gone for nearly a week, with broken bed rest and depressed surroundings, or if she signed any paper, there was something wrong with her. She could not have been mentally responsible. She has no recollection of having made any statement."[57]

Charlie Murphy also dropped by to see his sister, who had lost so much weight that he barely recognized the figure in the black dress as he approached her cell.

"I did not kill them, Charlie," Mary said, and tugged on his hands.

"I believe you," he said, his voice cracking. Tears ran down his cheeks.[58]

Charlie Murphy believed in his sister's innocence, but the bombardment of negative press had convinced readers of Mary's guilt. Women, captivated by the story of a caregiver who poisoned a baby, found the case particularly fascinating.

Boyd and Gilbert faced a public relations nightmare. Newspapers across the state detailed Mary's alleged confession. Several of these papers—the *Grand Rapids Post*, the *(Traverse City) Evening Record*, several Detroit dailies, the *Kalkaskian*, the *Kalkaska Leader* and the *Fife Lake Monitor*—circulated throughout

Kalkaska County. More troubling than the local papers, which ran weekly, were the out-of-town dailies from Traverse City, Grand Rapids and Detroit, which included daily news coverage of the case. All these publications included lists of other "suspicious deaths" in Mary's past. Several articles even categorized the deaths under subheadings as "known murders" and "possible murders."[59] Mary McKnight had been tried and convicted in the court of public opinion even before her examination took place.

Boyd tried to undo some of the damage. At first, he tried to pass off the confession as an invention of an overly imaginative newspaper reporter, but he was grasping at straws. Faced with the undeniable fact that his client made some sort of admission, he revised his position.[60] "No, I do not claim that Mrs. McKnight confessed," Boyd told a *(Detroit) Evening News* correspondent. "She made certain statements voluntarily, but she did not tell of any motive for her crimes. Do I think the court will admit her statement in evidence? Well, I expect it will be contested."[61]

By the end of the week, the controversy surrounding Mary's alleged confession caused Smith to do some spin control of his own. He reversed his earlier position when he told a reporter that Mary's statement couldn't really be called a confession, but he insisted that he didn't need it to make his case. Totten echoed the sentiments of his co-counsel: "As to the confession, the prosecution does not need it to prove this woman's guilt. The fact, however, that she repudiates the confession may have an important bearing on the case."[62]

Smith had to admit that the circumstances of Mary's so-called confession wouldn't meet muster with the courts and would never make it in front of a jury. So he hatched a plan. He wouldn't introduce the statement into evidence. Instead, he would put himself on the witness stand and testify as to what she said. His partner, William D. Totten, would handle the questioning.

Gilbert was thrilled when he heard about Smith's scheme. He was still stinging from Creighton's refusal to admit him into the jail to confer with his client, and Smith just handed him a way to even the score. He would handle the questioning for the defense.

As the date of the preliminary examination approached, Mary McKnight's mental and physical state further deteriorated. During her two weeks behind bars, she ate very little. Creighton described her diet to a shocked reporter for the *(Traverse City) Evening Record*: "She has a pineapple, of which she has eaten perhaps a third. On Sunday night she ate part of a small dish of strawberries. She has eaten about three of a dozen oranges she has had in her cell. That is everything that has passed her lips. She just says she does not care to eat." Creighton downplayed her weight loss. "She seems healthy enough," he noted, "and has not, apparently, lost flesh, but she complains of a bad headache."[63]

While she may have lost her appetite for food, Mary apparently didn't lose her appetite for connecting with people from the outside world now that Smith and Creighton allowed her to receive visitors. "Whatever she may lack in eating she makes up in talking," the *Evening Record* writer added, "for she is ready to talk to anyone whom she has the opportunity of seeing, and talks without stint."[64]

In the next day's edition, the *Evening Record* correspondent continued to describe Mary's demeanor, depicting the prisoner as confused and conspicuously religious, as if suffering from a guilty conscience: "She has her attorneys up in the air, as they do not know what to make of her various crochets of late. She is intensely religious these days, and wants a minister as often as he will call on her. She reads her bible a good deal and seems to feel satisfied with her relation to the deity."[65]

The press and the public alike continued to speculate about Mary's possible motives for murder. People just didn't believe the "mercenary motive"—John Murphy's life insurance policy and his forty-acre parcel of land—would have led to the death of three individuals. It hardly explained the murder of baby Ruth Murphy, and it certainly didn't explain any of the other victims Mary was suspected of killing. There had to be a darker motive, and people began to speculate that the murders came from a disturbed mind.

The rumors prompted Ernest Smith to address the media because insanity undermined the theory of the crime he and Totten planned to pursue at trial.

Smith told a *(Detroit) Evening News* reporter:

> *Mrs. McKnight may be demented, though I do not believe it. If I thought she were of unsound mind I would acknowledge it instantly. Whether sane or insane, though, she should be separated from the rest of society. The criticism that these murders could not have been planned for gain, and that therefore they reveal of their own force a disordered mind, does not seem to bear scrutiny. For one, I am not willing to conclude that a woman who will remove by poison a whole family in one week, and those persons blood-relatives, supposed to be dear to her, would balk at undertaking the deaths of a dozen more people in order to reach her ultimate goal.*[66]

Smith, however, didn't say what he believed was Mary's "ultimate goal."

As the date of the preliminary hearing approached, Mary McKnight became increasingly more despondent, falling into a deep depression. She penned a letter to her mother and handed it to Creighton to deliver. The sheriff, concerned about his prisoner's welfare, opened it. His mouth dropped open as he read the note:

> *I am so sick I can't live. I have wanted to die for a long time. The strychnine I sent for by Battenfield was for myself. I had made up my mind to take it, and would, only were sick, and then John died. I went out in the old home to take it, and you came in. It is fixed ready to take there, yet I could tell you just where to find it. After I had that last sick spell I made up my mind to end my own life, and not anyone else's. I wanted to die and get out of my suffering for some time. Don't believe I gave John anything, for it is out in the old house now.*

Mary then gave Sarah Murphy instructions for the dispersal of her property. "Put me by Willie," Mary said referring to her brother William's grave, "and be sure and have me embalmed. Don't take me to church but have it at the house. Pray for me as long as you live, the sooner I am dead the better." Mary ended the letter with a last request: "Get my white waist at Mrs. Barnes, put it on me; my clothes are Mrs. Jennison's."[67]

Creighton raced to the prosecutor's office. Winded, he dropped into a chair by the desk as Smith read the letter. The prosecutor decided to pay another visit to Mary's cell.

On the eve of the preliminary hearing, scheduled for June 17, Smith sat with Mary McKnight and listened to one, final confession. She told him that she had contemplated suicide and had purchased the poison for herself.

Meanwhile, Creighton took a carriage out to the Murphy place and did a sweep of the house. He found the strychnine pills exactly where Mary said she left them. To the sheriff, the discovery of the poison lent credibility to the story Mary wrote in her letter to Sarah Murphy. Mary sounded like a mentally unbalanced individual who planned to use the strychnine from Battenfield to "get out of" a longtime illness.

But to Smith, Mary's latest admission was just another feeble attempt to undo her statements about willfully giving her brother poison. She knew part of Smith's case hinged on her purchase of strychnine just days before John's death, and she knew Creighton would read her letter. So she fabricated a story to explain where it went.

The prosecutor had to hand it to Mary McKnight. It was a clever move. Creighton's discovery of poison on the Murphy farm could cast doubt on his theory of premeditation, and at the same time, Boyd and Gilbert could also use the letter to claim that Mary accidentally fed John Murphy a massive overdose of strychnine by giving him one of her loaded suicide capsules. Or they could use the letter as a prelude to an insanity plea. In reality, one of her relatives could have easily planted the strychnine in the house.

Although Smith was almost certain Mary's suicide note was a pretrial ploy, he ordered precautions to make sure Mary McKnight would not cheat the hangman. Sheriff's deputies pulled the shoestrings off her shoes. They removed the pen and inkwell that she used to write letters. And Creighton decided to have someone check on her every hour around the clock.

Meanwhile, the four attorneys prepared for a battle royal in justice court. Smith and Totten felt confident in their evidence but knew that they faced a formidable opponent. Former prosecuting attorney Joshua Boyd had defended the accused in the only two murder trials in county history.

Boyd's right hand was a fiery, competitive attorney who hated to lose and had an axe to grind with the prosecuting attorney. Thanks to Smith's clever gambit to sneak Mary's so-called confession through the back door by putting himself in the witness box, Parm Gilbert would have a rare chance to grill the prosecuting attorney about his tactics. Gilbert couldn't wait to cross-examine Smith and force him to defend his draconian treatment of Mary McKnight. But he would have to wait a week for his courtroom vendetta.

Joshua Boyd asked the court to delay the proceedings. Smith later explained that "Mr. Boyd and Mrs. McKnight" wanted "the arraignment postponed until a certain newspaper reporter who was in town had left."[68] The court consented and rescheduled for June 25.

9
Examination

KALKASKA COURTHOUSE, KALKASKA, MICHIGAN
Thursday, June 25, 1903

By June 25, Mary had become so weak that Sheriff Creighton carried her from the carriage into the court, where a newspaper reporter helped her to her seat. Most of the spectators in the gallery were women, moved by a morbid curiosity in the proceedings. None of them had ever witnessed a murder trial. A reporter from the *(Traverse City) Evening Record* described the accused, dressed as if for a funeral: "Her dress is of deep mourning, black hat, black gloves, black veil and a large black boa colarette around her neck."

Mary sat facing the audience but couldn't bear to look at the faces of former friends, neighbors, relatives and the curious who gathered in the justice court of Alfred Kellogg to listen to testimony. The *Evening Record* correspondent described Mary's demeanor: "The accused sat with her head bowed down during the hearing, which seemed to drop lower as it progressed, her handkerchief to her eyes and her eyes closed."

The writer added a barb: "She has always been an unsociable woman and made very few friends, and this seems to count against her on all sides."[69]

Prosecutor Smith called Joseph G. Battenfield to the stand first. As the only witness to John Murphy's death other than the accused, Battenfield was a linchpin in the case against Mary McKnight.

After questioning Battenfield about his relationship with the Murphy family, Smith asked him to recount what he saw in the upstairs bedroom of the Murphy farmhouse on the evening of May 2.

"As I was coming up the stairs, John says, 'Hold me down.' That was all."[70]

"Did you act on his request to hold his limbs down?" Smith asked.

"Well, yes, I put my right knee against his right knee, but I did not notice that his limbs attempted to come up, at all."

"How long did this convulsion last?"

"It was just a minute. Almost like a moment, a few moments at least. His face relaxed and he was gone."

"How long would you say it was he lived after you come?"

"It might have been five minutes, and it might have been three. I did not take any note of it, but I could not bring myself to believe that he died so quick. I would not be positive, but it was a very short time."

"Did the muscles relax after death?"

"They seemed perfectly ridged [sic] that evening."

"Did you assist in bathing and dressing him?"

Battenfield nodded. "I did."

"Were his muscles relaxed at this time?"

"You mean that they were limber?"

"Yes."

"No, sir, perfectly rigid."

With the details of John Murphy's final moments on record, Smith questioned the witness about the poison Mary asked him to buy in Fife Lake.

"Do you remember three or four days previous to this doing an errand for Mrs. McKnight?"

"I do."

"Can you say the nature of that, Mr. Battenfield?"

"Well, there was three requests. One was to bring the mail. Another to have the doctor stop. The third, was to bring her five cents' worth of strychnine."

"Did you get the strychnine?"

"I got the strychnine."

"Where abouts?"

"At LaBar's Drugstore."

"Where is that?"

"Fife Lake."

"Did she say anything about what she wanted the strychnine for?"

"Yes, she said there were mice in the cellar or cellar way, I think it was the cellar way, probably."[71]

Boyd stood and began his cross-examination. "Mrs. McKnight was there with him, was she not?"

"Yes, sir."

"She was doing all that she could for him?"

"Seemed to be, yes, sir, I think she was."

"You think you suggested the use of salt?" It was a key question. Although it was a vain attempt to save a dying man, if Mary gave John the salt or suggested that John take the salt, that fact would undermine the prosecution's attempt to show she deliberately murdered her brother.

Battenfield thought about it for a moment. "I think so," he said, "but I would not be positive in the use of the salt."

"Was it used?"

Battenfield nodded. "It was used. Yes, sir."

In addition to the salt, Battenfield said he also tried the camphor that Sarah Murphy asked him to bring. "I had pulled the cork out of the camphor bottle and put it to his nose. He said, 'It is no good, Joe, I am dying.' That was all. Just after that, he said, 'Hold me down, my feet will come right up.'"

Boyd ended his cross by questioning Battenfield about John Murphy's appearance. Once again, Battenfield described the victim's clenched fists and arched back. "His features were distorted and drawn out of shape," Battenfield added.[72]

Smith next called his medical expert, Dr. Perly W. Pearsall. The prosecutor focused his questions on Pearsall's observations about John Murphy's body. Pearsall explained that he and a crew exhumed Murphy's corpse from the Springfield Cemetery to remove the stomach.

"Describe the condition of his body from a medical standpoint," Smith said.

"The body was stiff. Rigor mortis had not left the body as yet."[73]

"Go on."

"Do you mean…"

"Did you notice anything about the position of his lower limbs?"

"The feet were drawn and instead of lying flat as they usually do in a dead body there [sic] were drawn. Both hands were somewhat drawn across the breast."

"Is this term rigor mortis coupled with the drawing in of the feet, normal condition of a dead body?"

"Not at the time, usually muscles relax and the body becomes limber."

In his next question, Smith summarized the characteristics of strychnine poisoning:

Dr., if a person died in a convulsion in which the symptoms were distortion of the face, the drawing back of the head, the clinching of the fists, the drawing up of the upper arms, the severe rigidity of all the muscles, and then being buried and exhumed within a period of a month, the muscles were still found to be rigid, rigor mortis still present, and the feet drawn inwards, would you be able from your experience of medicine to assign a probable cause of a person's death?

Boyd stood up and objected, but Kellogg allowed the question.

"Coupled with the history of preceeding spasms, growing in intensity with the post mortem evidences, I would be able to base an opinion."

"What do you mean by the previous history of preceeding convulsions?"

"Basing my opinion upon one convulsion alone would be hardly fact enough as to base an opinion as to the cause of death, but with the one convulsion and the post-mortem evidences a person would be able to base an opinion."

Smith asked the doctor's opinion as to John Murphy's cause of death.

"From my opinion," Pearsall concluded, "he died from the effects of irritant poison."

"What is an irritant poison?"

"Strychnine heads the list."[74]

Parm Gilbert stood from his chair and approached the witness box. Since Smith propped up Pearsall as an expert, Gilbert would use his line of questions to undermine the doctor's credibility.

"Well, Doctor," Gilbert began "you are what they call a homeopath, are you?"

Pearsall nodded and sat forward in his chair, ready for the barrage of questions about his professional opinion. "Yes, sir."

"You doctor principally with little white and pink pills, then," Gilbert quipped.

"Not altogether. No, sir."[75]

Gilbert prodded Pearsall about his experience with strychnine. The doctor admitted he had never treated a patient suffering from strychnine poisoning, but he said he saw it fed to a "large Newfoundland dog" in medical school. Flustered by Gilbert's belligerent tone, Pearsall stumbled to remember dates and times, making him appear shaky and unreliable. With a skillful sequence of questions, Parm Gilbert managed to throw Pearsall completely off balance.

After Pearsall left the hot seat, the court adjourned for lunch. Mary, who hadn't eaten an entire meal since her arrest four weeks earlier, sipped on a saucer of milk fortified with an egg yolk.

The afternoon session began promptly at 1:30 p.m.

Gilbert leered as the state's star witness against Mary McKnight—Ernest C. Smith—strode to the witness box. All eyes fell on the prosecutor, who would discuss what he and the press called Mary's confession. William Totten questioned his colleague.

Smith summarized his various interviews with Mary McKnight at the Murphy home in the weeks following John Murphy's death.

Totten asked him about Smith's interview with the accused on June 1. "Do you remember what was said?"

"Yes, sir," Smith replied. "She said again at the time of John's and Gertrude's and baby's death that there was no poison of any kind in the house except this mice poison she put out last winter. She said she had no poison of her own. Had not had any since last winter. She also said that at this time there was some antiseptic tablets in the house which probably contained poison." According to Smith, Mary repeatedly denied giving anything to her brother.

Smith went on to describe a visit he made to the Murphy house the next day. Mary adamantly denied giving John anything. "[Mrs. McKnight] said she wished to state that there was no poison of any kind in the house at the time of John's death excepting the afore said cornmeal poison and antiseptic tablets. She had none of her own. Had purchased none. [The q]uestion was then asked as to what she did with the Battenfield poison."

"What did she say?" Totten asked.

"She first said she had forgotten about it."

"Then what further?"

"Then said she now remembered of having sent by Mr. Battenfield for it. Said that was the strychnine she put in the cellar last winter. She then said she put it in the cellar in cornmeal two or three days previous to John's death."

"And do you recall what she then said, if anything?"

"She said she immediately emptied the Battenfield package of poison into a dish of cornmeal in the cellar. I ask[ed] her what for. She said to kill the mice."

Having established the fact that Mary changed her story about the presence of strychnine, Totten turned his line of questioning to Mary McKnight's admissions, which Smith had touted as a confession a few weeks earlier.

"Do you remember having a further conversation with her, Mr. Smith, concerning the same matter?"

"I do."

"Have you fixed the date?"

"June 8th in the jail."[76]

"What was said by her then relative to the same case?"

"She said that she did not put the Battenfield poison in the cellar. She did not open it until after John died. She put it in a capsule and put it in an old trunk at the old house. Intended to take it herself." Mary, it appeared, had become trapped in her own web of lies by offering several, differing explanations for the "Battenfield package of poison."

"Do you recall further what she said then?"

"Yes."

"You may state."

> *She said that the evening of John's death just before she retired he complained to her of having a pain in his side and of being quite nervous and he asked her if she had anything that would quiet his nerves. She said she told him she had some capsules she took to quiet her own nerves and told him they were up on top of her dresser on the cover of a little round box. For him to go and get them. She said John went upstairs and she is not sure whether he took one or two of them. He went to bed and she went to bed. Very soon he called her and was taken sick. I ask[ed] her what the capsules were. She said they were strychnine mixed with quinine. She had bought the strychnine and put it in quinine capsules. She had them fixed for her own use.*

"Do you remember whether she made further statement relative to the same matter?"

"Yes."

"You may state them?"

"I ask[ed] her if this capsule or capsules which John had taken were the same, from the same lot, that she gave to Gertrude."

"What was her answer?"

"She said they were."

"What further, if anything?"

"She said she did not intend to harm them."

"Said she did not intend to harm them?"

"Yes."

Totten then questioned the witness about the next night—June 9—when Mary McKnight admitted to giving poison to baby Murphy. Smith explained that the prisoner repeated much of the story she had told the previous night: how she gave capsules containing a strychnine and quinine mixture to both Gertrude and then John Murphy.

Smith paused and took a sip of water before continuing.

A few whispers broke the silence in the courtroom. Then when Smith put the glass of water down, the murmurs stopped. The women in the audience were most interested in Mary's alleged poisoning of the Murphy infant. A rustling from a light breeze passing through the trees outside the courtroom filtered in through the partially opened windows.

Boyd and Gilbert would scrutinize every word spoken by the prosecutor, who just two weeks earlier had proclaimed to the world that he had wrenched an admission of guilt from his prisoner—a confession he, and he alone, heard and that he, and he alone, scripted based on what Mary McKnight allegedly said. The defense attorneys would compare Smith's script with his testimony and look for any discrepancies.

"After she told me about John and Gertrude having strychnine," Smith explained, "I asked her what medicine the baby had. She said the baby did not have anything. I asked her if she did not remember of giving the baby anything. She said she did not. She had given the baby nothing."

The "confession" that Smith and Totten released to the press, which Mary supposedly signed and which newspapers across the state printed verbatim, omitted a key element of Mary's statement regarding the death of Ruth Murphy. The attorneys decided to use the preliminary hearing to set the record straight.

"That is the statement you wish to correct. State what occurred."

Boyd leaned forward, his weight resting on his forearms, and watched as Smith described Mary's admission about the child:

She related again the same as the first evening as to John and Gertrude and I asked her if she remembered anything about the baby. She said she did not. She asked me if I had heard from Ann Arbor. I had just received the telegram a few hours before and I handed it to her, stating that strychnine was found in the baby and Gertrude Murphy. I asked her again if she remembered anything about the baby taking any medicine. She said no, she could not remember. She finally said I do remember giving the baby a teaspoonful of water. I asked her what was in the water. She said she did not remember of putting something in the water. She then said the baby woke up and cried and that she wanted to put it back to sleep. She put some water in a glass and went into the pantry. She had a package of strychnine

and a package of anti febrim lying side by side on the pantry shelf. She
reached up and got one of the packages, opened it, and put a part of it in
the glass of water. Stirred it up and gave the baby a teaspoonful.

A few of the spectators gasped, which was followed by hushed murmurs from the gallery.

Smith continued, "She did not know whether she had the anti febrim or the strychnine package, but said, 'If there was strychnine in the baby's stomach, I must have got the strychnine.' She did not intend to harm either the baby, Gertrude, or John."

Gilbert and Boyd exchanged glances. Smith's testimony, they realized, didn't go far in proving Mary's guilt or innocence. But it was an admission that Smith's scripted "confession," which Mary allegedly signed, didn't capture the essence of her statement with regard to Ruth Murphy.

According to Smith's testimony, Mary said she accidentally mixed up medicines. She wanted to give anti febrim to the baby but grabbed the wrong package from the shelf, which contained poison. The wording of her signed "confession" suggested that she willfully mixed poison with water and spoon-fed the deadly concoction to the infant—the version repeated by newspapers throughout the state.

Totten ended his examination with one final question about what John supposedly said to Mary on his deathbed.

"During one of the interviews in the jail I asked her what John said while he was sick. She said he did not say a great deal. He exhibited a great amount of affection toward her. And aside from that he said, 'Mary, after I am dead, don't you ever let them dig me up.'"[77]

It was a convenient request, perhaps too convenient for the accused. Smith and Totten hoped the court would see it as Mary's attempt to block the exhumation of John Murphy.

Parm Gilbert, eager to begin questioning Smith, jumped out of his chair. The prosecutor thought he had outfoxed the defense by putting himself in the witness box, but Gilbert would try to make him look like a fool or worse. He would focus his line of questions on the incarceration of Mary McKnight. First, he would try to establish the duration of her isolation in the Kalkaska lockup. Then, he would use his line of questioning to rib Smith about not allowing him to see his client.

"How long a time was Mrs. McKnight kept in jail isolated from other people except yourself?"[78]

Smith denied Gilbert's accusation. "Not at all."

Gilbert grinned. "Now, Mr. Smith, you had her put in jail did you not?"

"I did not put her in." Smith smirked in a way that chafed Gilbert. The prosecutor was toying with him.

"By your orders?"

"Yes."

"Who else besides yourself had access to her cell?"

"The sheriff."

"Who else?"

"Mr. Boyd."

"At what time?"

"I do not remember now at what time. There was a couple of days, two or three, subsequent to her arrest when Mr. Boyd did not see her."

"It is not true that you had her put in jail on Sunday, the last day of May?"

"Yes."

"Is it not also true that you allowed no one except yourself and the sheriff to see her until the Wednesday evening of that week?"

"I do not remember but I think it was two or three days."

Irritated, Gilbert tried to pry an admission from the witness by reframing his question. "Let me see if you can recall this? Did you see a telegram coming from myself to her on Wednesday morning of that week?"

"I did not."

"Up to the time of the digging up of the other two bodies, you had given the sheriff orders to not allow anyone to see Mrs. McKnight, did you not? Alone, I mean."

"Alone?"

"Yes, alone or any other way."

"No, sir. I do not think so."

"What had you told him?"

"Why, up until the time she called for counsel and asked for counsel to come to her, my instructions to the sheriff was, he should allow no lawyer to breack [sic] in jail to see her."

Gilbert leered at Smith and shook his head in disbelief. He smiled. "Did you see any lawyer around with a jimmy trying to get the window up?"

"We saw many in the immediate vicinity."

A few women in the gallery chuckled. Gilbert wasn't amused.

Frustrated, Gilbert tried a different approach to track the number of days Mary McKnight was kept isolated from visitors. "At this day when you took the stomachs of the bodies to Ann Arbor, the second time you went down, did you tell the sheriff to admit no one except he [Sheriff Creighton] was present?"

"I think I did. Yes, sir, I think I did."

"How long did that rule apply in this case?"

"Why, I do not remember the date. It was sometime near the middle of the second week, if I am not mistaken."

"The second week of this month?"

"The second week of her stay in the jail. I do not just remember the date."

Gilbert realized an opportunity and used his next question to imply that Mary's so-called confession was coerced.

"You held to that rule until after you had obtained all of these conversations which you detailed, did you not?"

Totten objected, but Kellogg overruled. "Answer the question," he commanded.

Smith hesitated, unsure of his answer. "Why, no one was allowed to see her alone until after this statement, the last statement, that I have detailed here was made."

Gilbert's questions tongue-tied Smith and succeeded in casting suspicion over the treatment of Mary McKnight. Next, he turned his line of questioning to the atmosphere in the jail prior to Mary's alleged confession. The newspapers had reported that Smith prayed with the prisoner, brought her buttermilk and offered her a shoulder to cry on. Gilbert wanted to show that these kindnesses were in reality stratagems designed to gain Mary's confidence and lure her into making self-incriminating statements. The crafty defense attorney had already established that Smith silenced dissenting voices by isolating McKnight from both family and her lawyers.

"When did you [pray with her]?" Gilbert asked.

> *Later on. I took the clergyman over and she would ask me to read a chapter. I would read it to her, and she said, "Now, Mr. Smith, you are a Christian man, are you not?" I said, "I am." She prayed to the Lord, offered a prayer. She said, "Will you say something?" I certainly complied with a woman's request, and said a little something, the best I could under the circumstances. She usually, when I went over, would have a chapter marked and ask me to read it.*

Gilbert questioned Smith about the availability of food at the jail, since his client had wasted away under Creighton's care.

"She said she was unable to eat anything of any kind or description," Smith explained.

I asked her if she could think of anything she would possibly eat. She said some fresh buttermilk and she expected to have her sister, Mrs. Woodard, bring her up some. When I went home I told my mother the circumstance. My mother said she would send her over some. One evening she had some put up. I took it over and gave it to Mr. Boyd to take to her. I delivered it to him. I do not know whether he took it or not. I think he let it spoil before he took it over to her.

Boyd winced as if Smith's words jabbed him in the midsection.

"After coming from there at any time did you tell the newspaper reporter she fell on your neck and cried, as they have the case detailed here?"

"No, sir."

"If anything like that was published it was not any of your work?"

"No, sir."

"Was there ever any occurrence like that?"

"No."

Gilbert continued to prod Smith about his approach to the prisoner. "Did you at that time tell her, you were sorry for her, that your heart bled for her?"

"No."

"Did you any time prior to that say that to her?"

"I told the woman she was in a pitiable condition. That I pitied her."

"Did you not say to her and use these words? 'Mrs. McKnight, I am sorry for you. My heart bleeds for you.'"

"No, I do not think so."

"Will you swear you did not?"

"No, I do not remember about that conversation. I do not remember anything about saying that expression. I have told her on repeated occasions I was sorry for her and sympathized for her. It was enough to excite the sympathy of any man."

Gilbert was losing patience with the phrases—"I do not think" and "I do not remember"—that were coming from the witness box. "Now, Mr. Smith, is it not true you went to this woman on the different occasions, with this testament and in praying with her for the very purpose of getting her confidence to get her to talk to you?"

Smith sat forward and very slowly responded, "No."

"Why did you do it for?"

Smith explained:

Why, I went to the jail on the afternoon of June the 3rd, Sunday afternoon. The sheriff had told me that she was in a very much disturbed condition mentally. I told him I would go over and see how she was. I had not seen her previous to this time since Tuesday. Tuesday previous. I found her in a very nervous condition and in a condition which very much excited my sympathy toward her. I thought at that time that there must be some relief for the woman or else she could very soon lose her reason. I said to her: "Mrs. McKnight, I have not come to talk about the case in any way and I do not wish you to talk about it, I simply came to see how you were getting along." I said, "I presume you think because I am the prosecuting attorney, that I am necessarily an enemy of yours." I said, "Your condition excites my sympathy, and although I am the prosecuting attorney, if I can do anything to alleviate your sufferings I shall be glad to do it." I said to her, "If there is anything you want me to do, if there is any way in which I can help you, let me know and if I can do it, I will do so." I then said to her, "Have you ever been affiliated with any church?" She said she had once been a member or an attendant of the Baptist Church. And she asked me if there was a Baptist Church here in town. I told her there was and that I thought she would enjoy meeting the Baptist clergyman. She then asked me if I could bring him over. I told her I would. Would see him the next day and bring him over. Then she said to me, "I know you cannot be my attorney, but is there any reason why you cannot be a friend to me?" I said, "No, Mrs. McKnight, if I can do anything to alleviate your suffering, your present physical condition, I shall be glad to do so, but I want to have a fair and square understanding with you at this time." I said, "Mrs. McKnight, I have canvassed the situation from every stand point and have looked up the evidence from every stand point, and I cannot arrive at any conclusions possible, except that you administered the poison to John Murphy." I said, "If there was any possible doubt in my mind I would gladly give it to you, but I want to have a perfect and fair understanding with you right at this time upon that question." I said, "I have not come to talk with you about this case. You know what I believe about it and I cannot believe anything different." She made no reply. I arose to go and she said to me, "Well, I am glad you have come and I feel better. Will you come tomorrow and bring the clergyman?"[79]

Gilbert shifted his line of questioning to the alleged confession.

Smith recounted the evening of June 8. Boyd, he explained, was visiting his client in her cell until about 9:30 p.m.:

I sat down and waited until Mr. Boyd had gone. It was then at least 9:30. I thought I would not go up. The sheriff then told me that while he was leaving the cell with Mr. Boyd she had stopped him and whispered to him asking him if I had not come, saying to him she wished he would telephone me to come over. I then went up and the conversation as there mentioned [alleged confession] *took place. She said to me that she was in a very nervous condition and I could see also that she was and I said to her, "Mrs. McKnight, I believe you are carrying an awful weight upon you and that you will enjoy probably no peace of mind or quiet until you relieve yourself from it." I said, "I do not wish you to tell me anything." I said to her, "Of course, your attorneys have instructed you that you should not talk to me. I do not wish you to tell me anything regarding the case, but I do say to you that you will not find relief of your present mental condition until you unburden yourself to someone." She said, "I know I ought not to talk to you. Mr. Boyd has told me every day he has been here under no circumstances to have anything to say to you." But she says, "I am going to talk any way." And she related to me the circumstances of John's, Gertrude's death. I asked her no question of any kind regarding either one but when she had finished regarding these two I did ask her what kind of medicine the baby took. After she had made the statement which I have testified to again upon my leaving she said to me, "Will you come over again tomorrow." I told her I would if I could get away. She said, "I want to talk to you and I wish you could come over." I went over again the next night and she told me the further conversation that I have related. Since that time I have been over several times. She has sent for me a great number of times by the sheriff and I usually go whenever I can when she sends for me. I think that is all."*[80]

Smith then explained his scripting of his prisoner's statement:

After she had made this first statement that night of John and Gertrude's death[s], *I said nothing more to her when she denied having knowledge of the baby's death. The next night she told me regarding the baby's death. She protested her entire innocence of any guilty intent. However, she had told me the following conversation. I then said to Mrs. McKnight, "Have you any objections to my putting this in writing and your signing it?" I said, "You say you have given this strychnine without intent to harm any of these people." I said, "Do you want all the world to know how you claim that John and Gertrude and Baby Murphy come to their death." I said, "Do you want your people to know that?" She said, "It is true and I want them all to know." Then I wrote the statement and read it over to her and she signed it.*[81]

"Did you not at the time you speak of her making a written statement say to her that she ought to do that so you could show it to her brothers and sisters so they would know she was innocent?" Gilbert asked.

Smith nodded.

> *There was something said about showing the statement to her folks. I remember the conversation about whether she desire[d] to let them know whether these parties came to their death, and also as to her family and I remember of telling her that I would give out this statement just exactly as she made it including her statement that she did not intend to harm anyone, and she said, "All right," and that she wanted everyone to know these facts as they were stated at that time.*

"Was there any one else present except yourself?"[82]

"No one."

"I would like a direct answer to the question I put to you. Did you never say to her that you wanted her to sign that statement so that you could show it to her relatives to show that she was innocent?"

"No sir. I did not make that statement. I never told her once either directly or by an insinuation that I thought she was innocent."

With this last denial, Smith stepped down from the witness box and returned to his chair. He was sweating profusely. His shirt stuck to his back, and when a cool breeze whipped through the courtroom window, it sent a shiver down his spine.

Gilbert managed to sweat out of Smith the fact that on his orders, Creighton had kept Mary McKnight in virtual isolation until after she admitted to giving Gertrude and John Murphy poison. Everyone in the courtroom heard Ernest Smith stumble through a series of "I do not knows" and "I do not remembers," which made the prosecutor appear to be hesitant on certain points.

Gilbert called three additional witnesses to show that Smith and Creighton kept visitors from seeing Mary McKnight until after she made her alleged confession. Dan Murphy testified about his attempt to see Mary on June 1 and being turned away by Creighton.

"You may state whether there was an attempt made to visit her the next morning at the jail by you and me?" Gilbert asked.

"There was."

"Who did we talk with?"

"We talked with Creighton and the prosecuting attorney."

"We were denied the privilege of visiting your sister in the jail?'

"Yes, sir."

"Do you remember what was said by Mr. Creighton at that time?"

"No, I do not."

"Do you remember what was said by Mr. Smith, the prosecuting attorney, as to whether we could go over and visit her?"

"I think he said we could not."

Murphy went on to describe a heated discussion that he and Gilbert overheard among Boyd, Creighton, Totten and Smith about their refusal to allow access to Mary McKnight.[83]

Mary's sister Martha Woodard testified that she arrived in Kalkaska on Friday, June 5, and at that time, Creighton would not let her see her sister.

Undersheriff Alfred B. Cornell followed Martha Woodard. While Creighton and Smith were at the Springfield Cemetery exhuming the bodies of Gertrude and Ruth Murphy, he was in charge of the Kalkaska jail. On orders from Creighton, he denied Gilbert's request to visit with Mary McKnight.

Smith and Creighton left Justice Kellogg's court with black eyes, but Smith's strategy worked perfectly; his recollection of McKnight's statements was damning to her defense.

Nonetheless, Boyd and Gilbert moved for a dismissal and submitted a numbered list of five reasons. The third item on the list presented the court with an alternative version of John Murphy's death: "Because the proofs conclusively show that if John Murphy died from the effects of any poison the same was administered by his own hand."

The court rejected the motion to dismiss. Mary McKnight was headed to trial for the murder of her brother, but Parm Gilbert hoped it wouldn't take place in Kalkaska County. Local newspapers—the *Kalkaskian* and the *Kalkaska Leader*—in addition to dailies from Detroit and Grand Rapids, had circulated widely in Kalkaska County in the month following her arrest.[84] These publications flooded residents with front-page items that included neighborhood gossip and rumor. Just about everyone in the county had read Mary McKnight's alleged confession and had browsed lengthy lists of her other potential victims, which inflamed public opinion against her.

On a humid day in late August, Gilbert drafted an affadavit pleading for a change in venue. He turned to the typewriter in his office and began by indicting Smith and Creighton for their loose lips, noting that many of the damning statements were "apparently based upon reports and interviews given out by the prosecuting attorney of the county, and the sheriff of the county."

The substance and effect of these articles," Gilbert continued, "are that said Mary McKnight had murdered the entire Murphy family and that she had confessed herself to be guilty of murder; that she was a wholesale poisoner, and other articles were to the effect that the sheriff stated to the newspaper reporters that all of Mrs. McKnight's relatives and former friends and acquaintances had turned against her, being fully convinced of her guilt."[85]

Throughout August, Gilbert had canvassed residents of the county's various townships. He spoke to more than one hundred people and reached an alarming conclusion. "That local public feeling and sentiment is very strong against her in many neighborhoods and sections of the country," Gilbert said in pleading with the court to move Mary's trial from Kalkaska County. "The feeling [is] such that parties express a desire to see the respondent punished without any further hearing or trial."[86]

It appeared that some residents of Kalkaska wanted to spare the expense of a trial and take Mary McKnight to a tall tree for a little frontier justice.

Gilbert turned from the typewriter and ran his finger up a tower of newspapers sitting at the corner of his desk. He pulled one from the pile—the *Grand Rapids Post* from June 11—and scanned the headline: "Murderess M'knight Has Bad Record." Under a completely erroneous subtitle—"She Has Confessed to Three Murders"—the article categorized the deaths in Mary's history as "Suspicious" and "Not Suspicious."

Gilbert cringed as he read the last line in the article: "She told in detail how she administered the poison to Gertrude, her brother's wife, and when she died that John, her brother, was so badly broken up she thought it best that he should die and gave him the poison."[87]

He glanced at the stack of papers, which all contained parallel stories. He paused and massaged the bridge of his nose before returning to the typewriter. It would be impossible, he believed, to empanel an unbiased jury in Kalkaska County. Mary McKnight would not, could not, receive a fair, impartial trial there.

To prove his point, Gilbert submitted eighteen signed affidavits from citizens throughout the county stating that public opinion was so biased against Mary, any trial held there wouldn't be a fair one. The court agreed on a change of venue and relocated the trial to another county under the aegis of the Twenty-eighth Judicial Circuit. The biggest trial in the history of Kalkaska County would take place in neighboring Cadillac, the seat of Wexford County.

It was a victory for McKnight's defense team, but Gilbert doubted the change of venue would help his chances of securing a favorable jury.

MICHIGAN WOMAN ACCUSED OF
MURDER OF TWELVE PERSONS

MRS. MARY M'KNIGHT
TRIPLE MURDERESS

By the end of June, the Michigan Borgia had made nationwide news. This sketch appeared in the June 25, 1903 edition of the *Phillipsburg (Kansas) Herald*. *Library of Congress, Chronicling America, as provided by the Kansas State Historical Society.*

Newspapers from Detroit and Grand Rapids also circulated widely in Cadillac. At this point, Gilbert feared, he wouldn't find twelve people who hadn't read all about Mary McKnight when the trial began in mid-August.

As the trial date approached, Mary McKnight was on the verge of a mental and physical breakdown. Vilified in the press, convicted by the court of public opinion and condemned by many of her former neighbors, the once-attractive forty-six-year-old was a shadow of her former self. Even those who knew her remarked at how much her appearance had changed. She looked like she had aged years in a matter of weeks, and her weight dropped by nearly fifty pounds.

She became further distraught when her mother passed away on the evening of August 6. Sixty-seven-year-old Sarah Murphy died from "exhaustion following attack of bilious colic."[88]

Boyd and Gilbert visited their client in jail the next day. A few minutes with Mary convinced them that she was in no condition to stand trial, so they asked for a postponement.[89]

Boyd also wanted to ensure that four key defense witnesses—Dr. D.F. Stone, Mrs. J.T. Dalzell, J.C. Burton and Anna Jenson—could make it to the witness stand. In a letter to Boyd, Stone said it would be impossible to leave his patients, many of whom were suffering from life-threatening ailments such as typhoid fever. But if the trial took place in a few months instead, he promised to rearrange his schedule so he could appear in the witness box.[90]

The Kalkaska County courthouse, circa 1900. Because of the adverse news coverage, the McKnight trial would not be held in this building. *Author's collection.*

Mrs. Dalzell didn't respond to her subpoena. Boyd believed that she had moved but thought he could locate her if the court agreed to delay the trial.[91]

Nine months pregnant, Anna Jenson could not travel from Grayling to attend an August trial, and J.C. Burton was in North Dakota and wouldn't return for six weeks.[92] Boyd described all four of these witnesses as so important to the defense that "it will be unsafe for her to proceed to trial without" their attendance.[93]

The court honored Boyd's request. Northern Michigan's trial of the century would commence on November 30.

Carrie Collins looked in the mirror and wondered if the ordeal was taking its toll on her appearance. She had decorated her jail cell by hanging a mirror from a pair of stockings suspended from the ceiling bars.

As Mary McKnight's trial date approached, Caroline Collins—a thirty-nine-year-old widow who owned a farm near Hazelton—sat behind bars in the Shiawassee County jail for allegedly poisoning George Leachman, her hired hand.[94] Twenty-nine-year-old Leachman had lived at the Collins household, and according to local gossip, Leachman and Collins had a suspiciously close relationship. At about three o'clock on the morning of October 23, Leachman died in bed.

Initially, authorities believed his death stemmed from a drubbing he had received a week earlier. Leachman wrote a note containing some lecherous comments to a neighboring woman. When her husband found out about it, he and a few male relatives ambushed Leachman and pummeled him. Over the next few days, a local doctor treated his injuries, and when he died, his cause of death was presumed to be pneumonia that resulted from a weakened system.[95]

Furious, residents of Hazelton demanded justice, and Shiawassee County prosecutor William J. Parker opened an investigation. He had Leachman's body exhumed and asked local doctors Burke and Shoemaker to conduct a postmortem. During the autopsy, they removed the stomach and sent it to Ann Arbor for analysis. A chemist there discovered that Leachman's stomach contained arsenic, although not enough to have killed him.

Meanwhile, the rumor mill began to churn about the widow Collins and her hired man. People whispered about an alleged *affair de coeur* with Collins trapped in a love triangle between Leachman and Colonel John Northwood, a local lawyer and veteran who lost an arm in the Civil War. The widow wanted to marry the colonel, but Leachman was in the way. Collins also allegedly owed Leachman money.

While most of Carrie Collins's neighbors believed her innocent, Parker began envisioning a scenario in which the widow gradually poisoned her lover to make room for the colonel. He discovered that she nursed Leachman after the beating, and just days before his death, she purchased "Rough on Rats"—a pesticide containing arsenic.

As soon as they heard the word "arsenic," gossips began whispering about the other deaths associated with Collins.

Fears of another Michigan Borgia led Parker to exhume the body of Collins's nephew, Ira Wright. The thirteen-year-old lived with his aunt until his death on June 21, 1903, following a supposed bout with gastroenteritis, which shared symptoms—vomiting and diarrhea—with arsenic poisoning.[96] Once again, a small quantity of arsenic—one tenth of a grain—was discovered in the victim's stomach.

As Parker dug into Caroline Collins's past, he discovered yet another death. Collins's daughter, eighteen-year-old Ida May Weisenberger, died on December 19, 1902, just after giving birth to a daughter. Caroline Collins nursed Ida during her recovery.[97]

Whether the victims of murder or misfortune, the three people who lived in the widow's household in 1900—Leachman, Wright and Weisenberger—all perished within a year of one another. Prosecuting Attorney Parker was convinced it was more than an eerie coincidence.

People also began to wonder if Collins had poisoned her husband, Nicholas.

"A prominent Hazelton man today," wrote a reporter the same day Mary McKnight arrived in Cadillac for her trial, "told the *Detroit Free Press* that at the time N.B. Collins died of typhoid fever, as then given out, that there was no typhoid fever or other contagions or infectious disease within many miles of Hazelton."[98]

Carrie Collins answered the charges when a reporter for the *Corunna Journal* visited her at the county jail. He was quite impressed by the widow: "Mrs. Collins is of medium height and more than passably good looking. Moreover there is an air of refinement about her, and she is very intelligent. Her voice is low and soft. There is a wholesomeness about the woman which contrasts strikingly with one's preconceived idea of a cold-blooded murderer."[99]

Collins was in the middle of writing a letter but put down her pen to answer the correspondent's questions. His first question was about Leachman's cause of death.

This sketch of a "cage" appeared in the jail cell catalogue of E.T. Barnum's Iron Works, a Detroit manufacturer specializing in the construction of jail cells, fences and other wrought-iron products. Barnum installed similar cells in the Cadillac and Owosso jails around 1900. *Author's collection.*

"I don't know; I'm no doctor," Collins said in a matter-of-fact tone. "But I do know that after the beating the Burpees gave him, and the trouble he had about that letter, he was never the same. He was a man who got discouraged very easily. Why, he felt so bad about that Burpee matter that one morning he threatened to kill himself. Another day, I believe he would have done so, for he had a revolver with which to blow out his brains, and I got it away from him only after considerable trouble."

Next, the reporter asked about the arsenic she allegedly possessed:

> *Did I ever have any rough on rats around the house? Never but one box. Did Leachman ever have any poison? No, I never saw him have poison. He might have got it one day when we went to Chesaning together. That was a couple of weeks before he died. When he got home he complained of being sick. He didn't eat any supper, nor any breakfast. He tried to drink a glass of milk but vomited afterwards that morning. George's health was never rugged. The day mother went to Gladwin, Sept. 30, I think he was at Montrose, and he might have bought some stuff then.*

Turn-of-the-century county jails, like this one in Gratiot County constructed in 1879, typically contained a sheriff's residence on the first floor and cells on the second floor. The E.T. Barnum Iron Works, based in Detroit, built cages for many of Michigan's early jails.

During her trial in Cadillac, Mary McKnight, spent time in one of Barnum's cages. The Owosso county jail, where Caroline Collins was held pending her trial, also used Barnum's jail cells. *Author's collection.*

Finally, the reporter asked her if she had anything to do with the death of Ira Wright. She replied, "No indeed. I took him to raise when he was five months' old, and I was good to him. He seemed to take Mr. Collins' place since my husband died, four years ago, and had pretty much his own way around the place."[100]

As Caroline Collins crocheted away the hours in the Shiawassee County jail and Mary McKnight boarded the GR&I rail line in Kalkaska, a thirty-three-year-old farmer's wife strolled into a Big Rapids pharmacy to purchase five cents' worth of strychnine. Emma Stewart's husband, George, wanted it to kill the rats that had nested in their granary. The couple ran a farm about five miles from Big Rapids.

Mecosta County jail as it would have appeared in December 1903, when the county prosecutor debated about whether to charge Emma Stewart with the murder of her husband. *Author's collection.*

George Stewart waited in the carriage as his wife bought the poison. Earlier that evening, he had downed almost an entire bottle of whiskey, which left him nearly comatose.

Later that night, Stewart suffered from a sequence of convulsions. He died at nine o'clock on the morning of December 1, 1903.

His death didn't surprise many, least of all his doctor. The forty-year-old farmer was known as a heavy drinker. Just ten days earlier, he had drunk himself into such a stupor that Emma summoned Dr. Curtiss, who prescribed medicine for "an irritation of stomach caused from alcohol." Based on the victim's history, Curtiss concluded that George Stewart died from "alcoholic excess."[101]

Then the gossip started. People whispered about Stewart's drunken behavior and speculated that his wife found a way to rid herself of her sot husband. They learned Emma Stewart purchased strychnine the same evening her husband became sick and died. Newspapers across the state carried stories about the pending McKnight trial, and like the residents of Shiawassee County, they, too, pondered the possibility of another Michigan Borgia on their doorstep.[102]

At the request of Big Rapids prosecutor Joseph Barton, local doctors conducted a postmortem and discovered a large amount of strychnine in George Stewart's stomach. A sweep of the Stewart residence led to the discovery of a strychnine package with two grains missing.

Emma Stewart was in big trouble.

Part 3

The People v. Mary McKnight

10

The Trial of the Century[103]

CADILLAC, MICHIGAN

Tuesday, December 1–Friday, December 4, 1903

News correspondents from across the state joined the throng at the rail depot in Cadillac, Michigan, on Monday, November 30, as the southbound train pulled into the station. Over three hundred faces, eager to catch a glimpse of the alleged mass murderess, crowded the platform. They expected to see the plump, sinister spinster depicted by the press, but instead a frail, sallow-cheeked, hunched-over figure emerged from the train. A chorus of "oohs" broke the silence as Mrs. McKnight steadied herself by clinging to the arm of her sister Margaret Chalker.

The *Detroit Tribune* reporter, who signed his articles "NATHAN," described the pathetic character's grand entrance in Cadillac: "Almost as yellow as parchment, the heavily wrinkled skin hanging loosely from her face, her frame shriveled and bent, this woman whose alleged crime has almost no parallel in the history of the criminal courts, is helped about by two people as she cannot stand alone."[104]

In a feeble attempt to avoid the gawkers, she kept her eyes closed as the Chalkers escorted her through the crowd. "She is physically a wreck, and mentally on the verge of collapse," Nathan observed as Mary McKnight and her escorts shuffled past.[105]

Cadillac street scene, circa 1900. Next to the Hotel McKinnon is a liquor store. Blue laws banned the sale of liquor on Sundays, unless the merchant was a "druggist." The case immediately preceding the McKnight trial involved Peter Anderson, a saloonkeeper who sold booze on a Sunday. *Author's collection.*

A *Grand Rapids Herald* writer also watched Mary McKnight descend onto the train platform. He was shocked by the character that emerged from the train. The infamous Michigan Borgia didn't look like a monster capable of a triple murder. He described Mary as "a pitiable sight. She is haggard and pale and looks as if every hope has fled."[106]

The next morning, deputies escorted the emaciated Mrs. McKnight from her jail cell to the Wexford County courthouse. At just after nine o'clock, Judge Clyde C. Chittenden entered the courtroom, and the morning session got underway with jury selection.

Smith and Gilbert took turns questioning potential jurors. Gilbert focused his questions on which news items of the case each man had read, "openly conveying the impression that certain published accounts were either prejudicial to their client or erroneous in the statements they contained," Nathan noted.[107]

Chittenden listened, his palms pressed together and his fingers to his lips as if in prayer, while the attorneys quizzed each man. He glanced at the defendant, who sat with her head drooped. As she did at the preliminary hearing, Mary wore a black veil that covered her face. In his three years on the bench, Chittenden hadn't seen a more pathetic sight than the shadow of a woman sitting between Joshua Boyd and Parmius C. Gilbert. Chittenden had presided over the trials of con artists, train robbers and murderers but nothing like the case of Michigan's Borgia.

The son of a New York farmer and Civil War veteran, Chittenden practiced law in his native state before moving to Michigan in 1883. He ran a private practice in Cadillac until he began a long career in public service by winning election as a circuit court commissioner. In 1886, he became Wexford County's prosecuting attorney, beginning the first of three terms.

Chittenden moved to Michigan when the lumber industry in the Lower Peninsula was in full swing, and he made a fortune investing in it. While serving as the county's top lawman, Chittenden went into business with a local lumberman, George E. Herrick. A few years later, he and his father bought out Herrick and opened the Chittenden Lumber Company, which specialized in the transportation of logs. Chittenden divided his time as county prosecutor and company vice-president. Meanwhile, the business flourished. The company opened mills and built a railroad—the Osceola and Wexford line—used to move logs from the forests to their mills at Hoxeyville.

In 1894, the lawyer-turned-lumber baron ascended to the state legislature as a senator, and in 1900, he was elected judge for the Twenty-eighth Judicial Circuit Court, which serviced several northern Michigan counties, including

Train lines, built to move timber from the lumber camps to the mills, crisscrossed northern Michigan in the early twentieth century. *Library of Congress.*

Kalkaska and Wexford. He earned a reputation as a tough but impartial judge. Residents didn't think twice about bringing their problems to Judge Chittenden, who had a knack for settling disputes.[108]

Jury selection took the entire morning session of Tuesday, December 1. The lawyers grilled forty-three men and managed to select twelve before Chittenden adjourned for the noon break. Two officers—Undersheriff Ed Paquette and Deputy Sheriff John Torrey—escorted the jurors out of the courtroom and kept an eye on them during the break.

Since inaccurate and inflammatory news articles had already led to a new trial date, a change of venue and a major ordeal empanelling a jury—a fact Parm Gilbert made during the morning session—Judge Chittenden wanted to make sure the media didn't mar the fairness of this trial. He told the jurors that the court would supply newspapers for them to read during breaks as long as the McKnight case wasn't mentioned in any of them. Paquette and Torrey spent most of the morning session poring through local papers, pulling off front pages and slicing out columns.

When the court reconvened at 1:30 p.m., the prosecution opened its case. Smith outlined his theory of the crime: Mary McKnight, he explained, murdered her brother in an attempt to acquire his forty acres and his $1,000 insurance policy. In the days leading up to the murder, she fraudulently tripled the mortgage from $200 to $600. She first did away with John Murphy's beneficiaries—Gertrude and Ruth Murphy—and then her brother. With the family gone, she could foreclose on the property. Following John Murphy's death, Mary put her plan into action. She brought the raised mortgage to the county offices for recording—her first step in legally acquiring the property—and then made inquiries about his insurance policy.

After describing Mary's diabolical plot, Smith called a sequence of witnesses to show that John Murphy died from an overdose of strychnine. Joseph Battenfield repeated much of what he said at the preliminary hearing. He described John Murphy's last moments and the appearance of his body when he helped prepare it for burial. He also testified about purchasing strychnine for Mary in Fife Lake.

Undertaker William Wilson followed Battenfield and gave a detailed description of his embalming methods. Smith needed the undertaker's testimony to counter a possible defense argument that the presence of poison in John Murphy's stomach was the result of the embalming process, since the fluid commonly used by mortuaries contained strychnine. Wilson explained that he inserted embalming fluid only into the abdominal cavity and not the internal organs.[109]

John Jors, the cemetery sexton who took part in the exhumation of John Murphy's remains, testified next. In graphic detail, he described the curled-up body exhumed that frigid day at the Springfield Cemetery.

Dr. Perly Pearsall took the stand after Jors. He explained how, in cases of strychnine poisoning, rigor mortis was prolonged and how John Murphy's corpse was a textbook example. Several jurors—ten of the twelve were farmers—nodded when Pearsall said Murphy's hands were bent upward somewhat like a man holding the reins of a horse. A few of the jurors winced when Pearsall described removing Murphy's stomach, lungs and liver.

Gilbert cross-examined Pearsall, who shocked Smith when he said that a person's system could become accustomed to strychnine. By gradually increasing the amount taken, Pearsall said, a person could eventually consume an amount that would normally be fatal.

Pearsall's testimony, Smith realized as he listened to the cross-examination, could potentially dynamite the prosecution's case. The defense wanted to show that if Mary willfully gave John capsules containing strychnine, she accidentally gave him too much. By her own admission, she took a quinine and strychnine concoction to calm her nerves. If she had become accustomed to larger and larger doses, and she fed John one of her pills to soothe his nerves that night, then Murphy's death could have been nothing more than a tragic accident. The prosecution's own witness had presented the jury with a scenario in which Mary didn't murder her brother. Smith would rely on his next witness to show the jury what he knew to be fact: the massive amount of poison in Murphy's system left little doubt that his death was no accident.

When Gilbert finished with Pearsall, Smith called Dr. Ernest D. Reed.

Dr. Reed, who made the trek northwest from Ann Arbor, discussed the effects of strychnine on the central nervous system. He described how the victim would struggle for breath. The victim's back would bow and his face would become contorted. His lips would be pulled back into a forced grin. And his body would remain rigid long after death, just like John Murphy's.

Reed knew the perfect way to illustrate the effects of the massive strychnine overdose John Murphy had ingested. He held up a vial that, he said, contained poison removed from Murphy's stomach. With the court's permission, he would dose a frog, and the jury could witness the deadly effects of the strychnine remaining in the victim's stomach.[110]

Boyd jumped out of his chair and objected.

The sun had dropped below the horizon, so Chittenden adjourned with Boyd's objection unanswered. The judge wanted to sleep on it and make a decision at the beginning of the next day's session.

"The afternoon session closed with Reed on the stand," a reporter for the *Grand Rapids Herald* noted. "Tomorrow morning he will give a scientific demonstration before the jury."[111]

The morning session of December 2 began with a strong objection from Joshua Boyd, who didn't want the jury to see a frog croak. Chittenden agreed and sustained Boyd's objection. When the audience heard the decision, an audible groan erupted from the gallery, prompting Chittenden to tap his gavel until the grumblings dissipated.

Smith devoted the morning session to expert medical testimony. He would recall Dr. Reed to the stand, but first, he wanted to undo the damage caused by Dr. Pearsall the day before.

Mary watched, her face covered with a black veil, as Dr. Pearsall returned to the witness box. A *Grand Rapids Herald* writer described the defendant: "The prisoner sat throughout the day steadfastly looking at the floor with frequent spells of head shaking. She is attended by her sisters."[112] *Detroit*

Tribune writer Nathan described Mary as sitting "with her head bowed as usual, and with her fingers to her ears, presumably, to prevent her hearing any of the testimony."[113]

Mary's two sisters sat behind her, Mrs. Chalker to her right and Mrs. Woodard to her left. Nathan noted the demeanor of Martha (Murphy) Woodard, Mary's youngest living sister. She did not exchange a single word with Mary. According to Nathan, Martha once declared that she would not speak to Mary until she was proven innocent.[114]

Pearsall contradicted his previous testimony by stating that a person could take only a maximum dosage of strychnine and that that maximum amount depended on a person's physical state. This new testimony led to a sharp exchange between Pearsall and Gilbert, who wanted to know how the doctor could reverse his previous statements.

Pearsall explained that after he left the courthouse yesterday, he had read about strychnine in the medical literature. He also spoke with other physicians about it last night and subsequently changed his mind.

Gilbert was furious. He suspected Pearsall's new expert opinion resulted from a conversation with the prosecution's other expert witnesses. He glared at the doctor. Realizing there was nothing he could do about Pearsall's change of heart, Parm Gilbert returned to his seat.

Dr. Reed followed Pearsall. He said he extracted five-sixths of a grain of strychnine from John Murphy's stomach. The medicinal dose was between one-thirtieth and one-sixtieth of a grain, Reed explained, but it wasn't this quantity that killed John.[115] The amount absorbed in the blood, which subsequently traveled to the brain and spinal cord, caused the deadly convulsions. The massive amount of strychnine found in John's stomach only hinted at a much larger quantity swallowed. That much poison in John Murphy's system made it impossible to believe his death was an accident. And it precluded the possibility that it was injected as part of the embalming process. Reed also said he did not find any trace of quinine in John Murphy's system.

The chemist's testimony crippled Mary's defense in more ways than one. Boyd and Gilbert wanted to plant the idea that the presence of strychnine resulted from the undertaker's activities. And Mary claimed that she gave John some of her medicine and that he must have accidentally taken one too many, but her tablets contained both strychnine and quinine.

Next on the stand was Professor A.M. Clover, an instructor in the University of Michigan's Chemistry Department and one of the experts Smith called on to help him make his case. He showed the jury a vial containing strychnine removed from the liver and kidneys of Ruth Murphy and testified about the overdose she ingested.

The afternoon session was dominated by the testimony of Charlie, Dan and James Murphy. Smith wanted to show the jury, through witnesses intimately familiar with the place, that the Murphy homestead did not have a population of mice. And thus, Mary didn't have a need to acquire poison for that purpose.

The prosecutor's strategy backfired when the brothers Murphy rallied around their sister. All three testified about John Murphy's debilitating asthma. He would suffer from a smothering sensation, they said, usually just after he went to bed. These spells left him gasping for breath. His hands clenched, he would claw at the air like a man drowning on land. Only after he downed a few capsules of medicine he took for this condition did he begin to relax.[116]

Smith asked each brother if Mary said she gave John the medicine he took the night he died. All three brothers denied hearing such a statement. James Murphy testified that Mary told him John died during one of his fits of asthma. She said she fanned John and gave him water but no medicine.

James Murphy also testified that when Mary told him about his brother's death, she said John's last request was "'Have them bury me near Willie, and don't let them dig me up.'"[117] Mary made a similar statement when Creighton arrested her. At the time, Smith believed she fabricated John's last wish in order to prevent an exhumation, but James's testimony provided corroboration that made Mary's statement appear more plausible.

Charlie described John's affectionate relationship with Mary. He said he could never believe Mary guilty of murder unless confronted with unshakeable proof. He also said he used some of the strychnine at the Murphy house to poison a dog that was on its last legs. This last bit of testimony indicated that Mary McKnight had ready access to strychnine, but it also proved that John did, too.

The testimony of the Murphy brothers presented the jury with an alternative to the coldblooded murder that Smith depicted in his opening statement. If John took strychnine on a regular basis for his asthma, it was possible that he accidentally, or purposefully, took too much.

The press characterized it as "a red letter day" for the defense.

Interest in the McKnight trial remained high throughout the third day, Thursday, December 3. Curious observers packed into the gallery of the courtroom. "Every nook and corner of the stuffy little courtroom is occupied during every session," noted the *Traverse City Daily Eagle* correspondent with a tone of irritation, "women stand on chairs, on the window sills and in every possible corner where a footing may be received."[118]

The third day of the prosecution's case was focused on the testimony of two witnesses: Sheriff John W. Creighton and Prosecutor Ernest C. Smith.

During his testimony, Creighton described the various and contradictory statements Mary made. First, she denied there was any strychnine in the house, except for a small quantity placed in the cellar earlier that winter. Then, when confronted about the poison she purchased through Battenfield, she changed her story and said she put this poison in the cellar for the rats. Mary, Creighton explained, contradicted herself again when she penned a letter to her mother and told Sarah Murphy where in the house she kept capsules of strychnine. Creighton read the June 15 letter aloud.

Creighton also said he heard Mary McKnight repeat the confession she made to Ernest Smith in the Kalkaska jail.

With his cross-examination, Boyd wanted to show the jurors that the so-called confession was coerced.

Through his skillfully crafted line of questions, Boyd got Creighton to admit that he kept Mary McKnight in virtual isolation for three to four days, allowing her to see only himself and the prosecutor. During the entire first week of Mary's imprisonment, even her relatives were denied access.

Fidgeting on the witness stand as Boyd fired one question after another at him, Creighton blushed when he admitting to making several critical comments about Mrs. McKnight. On one occasion, when Mary pounded on the bars of her birdcage, he threatened to throw her into a dungeon "if she didn't stop that damned noise."[119]

Boyd ended his cross-examination by asking Creighton to rehash Mary's explanation about the pills. Mary, Creighton testified, repeatedly said that when John felt bad, she told him where to find capsules containing strychnine and quinine. She told John these would help him and that she believed they would not harm him.

As the sheriff slowly stood up and stepped down from the witness box, Ernest Smith walked to the stand. Once again, the prosecutor would become his own star witness.

Smith wanted to read the confession he penned by proxy, but Gilbert objected. Chittenden sustained the objection but did allow the signed document into evidence. Smith handed it to the clerk and then recalled Mary's statements from June 8 and June 9. When he described Mary's admission to giving strychnine capsules first to Ruth and then to Gertrude Murphy, several of the ladies in the audience gasped. "I don't think she meant to admit that she had committed any offense," Smith added.[120]

Parm Gilbert handled the cross-examination. He quizzed Smith about his role as attorney for Gladys Murphy. Smith sheepishly admitted that he did represent the girl in her battle to inherit John Murphy's land, which was allegedly owned by James Murphy. It was an important piece of testimony for Mary's defense. As a claimant for John Murphy's estate, Gladys stood in front of Mary McKnight, which undermined the prosecution's theory that Mary murdered for money. And if James did in fact hold title to the land, then murdering John didn't necessarily put Mary in a position to acquire the property.

After three hours of testimony followed by intense grilling from Gilbert, Smith stepped off the witness stand, and the court adjourned for the day.

By the end of the trial's third day, it became evident that Boyd and Gilbert were trying to show the poisoning of John Murphy was accidental. So Smith would counter by focusing the testimony of the trial's fourth day—Friday, December 4—on the deaths of Ruth and Gertrude Murphy. He would attempt to prove that Mary knew about the deadly effects of strychnine poisoning before she gave John his "medicine."

That evening, Joshua Boyd read through a copy of the *Grand Rapids Herald* morning edition. He wanted to see how the daily that had crucified his client in its June coverage of the case perceived the day's doings in court. He found an item under the page-two section "News in Michigan." Boyd scowled as he read the headline "CONFESSION OF MRS. M'KNIGHT," which detailed Smith's testimony. Even though Chittenden wouldn't allow Smith to read the alleged confession, the jury heard all about it, which the *Herald* reporter characterized as "damaging."[121]

The next column contained an article about the exhumation of John Ludwick in Bronson and the cloud of suspicion hanging over his widow for allegedly poisoning him. Boyd hoped that the officers watching over the jury would keep that item from their view. News of a parallel poisoning case could only hurt his client.

Boyd's heart sank when he read a small item about a massive fire that ravaged Hillsdale. He had been so tied up with the McKnight case that he hadn't had the time to keep current on the news back home. He thought of the hours spent, alongside his father, hammering away at wooden beams as they built many of the buildings in Hillsdale.

He rubbed the calluses covering his hands. What took many long, hard days to construct took mere minutes for fire to destroy.

Boyd glanced at the kerosene lantern and wondered if the Hillsdale inferno started when someone accidentally knocked over such a lamp. Within the next few years, electric light bulbs would make the flammable lanterns obsolete. Already, electric lines had begun appearing above main streets across Michigan. It was only a matter of time before all towns were wired.

One other item caught the attorney's eye: a humorous bit under the title "WOMAN TERRORIZES SALOON." A resident of Constantine named L.D. Cond liked to tip the bottle at local saloons. In fact, he liked to frequent taverns so much that his wife, Kitty, demanded the village saloonkeepers cut him off permanently.

When her husband didn't return home one evening, she went looking for him, only to find him tipsy on a barstool at William Withers's saloon. The inebriated patrons giggled when Kitty clenched onto Cond's ear and yanked him off the stool and out of the establishment.

Giggles turned to gaping mouths when Mrs. Cond returned with a loaded revolver. The revelers dove behind a large potbelly stove and under tables as Kitty pointed her gun at the large mirror hanging behind the bar. She didn't have the strength to squeeze the trigger, so she regripped the pistol with both hands and fired five times. The bullets shattered the mirror, raining glass shards on top of Withers. Boyd chuckled as he read the article. He bet that no saloonkeeper would ever serve L.D. Cond again.

Then Boyd reread the headline about the McKnight case, and his smile disappeared.

As the court convened on the morning of December 4, 1903, people crammed into the Wexford County courthouse to hear testimony about the poisoning of a young mother and her infant daughter.

The morning session began with two witnesses whose testimony severely damaged Mary McKnight's defense. The first to testify was Mary Mullen, who stated that she received the package of strychnine from Battenfield and placed it on the kitchen table. A few minutes later, it was gone. She also said she witnessed Mary McKnight feed a pill to Gertrude Murphy, who suffered from a convulsion within minutes.

Gilbert cross-examined Mullen. He asked each question very slowly—a cue about Mullen's mental age he hoped the jurors would recognize—but despite his repeated efforts, he could not shake her testimony. Mullen insisted she saw Mary McKnight pop a pill into Gertrude's mouth.

Next, Smith called Mrs. Sarah Dine to the stand. She said she stood alongside Mary Mullen and watched Gertrude Murphy's final moments.

Just after Gertrude took her last breath, Mrs. Dine said she heard McKnight say, "I know this will kill poor John inside of two weeks."[122] Ten days later, John Murphy was dead.

Once again, Gilbert tried to undo the damning testimony during his cross-examination. He wanted the jury to see his client as a caregiver who erred in her judgment by accidentally overdosing her victims, so he asked the witness to recall another statement she overheard. Mrs. Dine said that when Mrs. McKnight was asked if she had something to calm Gertrude's nerves, she responded, "No, not unless I give her one of my own capsules."[123]

After Mrs. Dine, Creighton returned to the stand and testified that McKnight admitted giving poison to the Murphy infant. Following the sheriff's second trip to the witness box, the court adjourned for lunch.

The sensational case caught the attention of local domestics and housewives, who queued up to catch a glimpse of Mary McKnight in court, moved by a morbid fascination of the woman who committed the ultimate sin when she murdered baby Ruth Murphy. "Interest in the trial," wrote a *Grand Rapids Herald* correspondent, "is unabated and it is necessary to station officers in the corridors to keep the crowd back. Women predominate in the audience, and today several brought their dinners and stayed through the noon intermission in order to hold their seats."[124]

After the noon break, Smith called a chain of witnesses to show Mary McKnight's motive for murdering the Murphy family. Smith admitted into evidence John Murphy's life insurance policy in the amount of $1,000 and the mortgage document that triggered the investigation. Justice of the Peace Alfred Kellogg explained to the jury that he had helped prepare the document in 1899, but it wasn't recorded until May 7, 1903—just five days after John's death and with the mortgage figure suspiciously raised from $200 to $600.

Smith recalled Dr. Reed, who testified about the amount of strychnine found in the stomachs of Ruth and Gertrude Murphy. He said there was no way it came from Wilson's embalming. Clover followed Reed and seconded his colleague's opinion. The strychnine found in the two victims, Clover insisted, did not come from the process of embalming.

With the testimony of the Ann Arbor scientists, Smith concluded his case, and the afternoon session came to a close.

The Case for the Defense

CADILLAC, MICHIGAN

Saturday, December 5–Tuesday, December 8, 1903

As Parm Gilbert approached the jury box to give his opening statement on Saturday afternoon, December 5, he felt good about his case. Smith had utterly failed to prove motive. It was a stretch to believe Mary snuffed John Murphy over forty acres and $1,000, especially since she had several times that much in the bank from the insurance policies of her deceased husbands.

And with his cross-examinations, Gilbert underscored the possibility that the poisonings were accidental.

Mary, Gilbert would argue, gave her brother medicine to help him, not harm him. Charlie and Dan Murphy—both witnesses for the prosecution—helped the defense when they testified about John's debilitating asthma attacks and his history of taking capsules to ease his symptoms.

Gilbert stood in front of the jury box and began his opening statement:

> *In the main, the defense will claim that whatever occurred in the Murphy home on the occasion in question, occurred in the ordinary course of events of the household, and that if any poison was given to anyone of those persons, there was no more criminal intent, no more intention to kill John Murphy than there is an intent on the part of any of you gentlemen to do any such thing. We will bring in evidence to show you something of the*

life of this woman, of the good reputation she has always borne. We shall insist that if she gave anyone any medicine, it was only what she was using herself, and had used time and again without injury, and she had no idea of destroying her brother John. We will show his condition. How he had ailed for years. We will also claim that statements made by her from time to time were made under such circumstances and under such surroundings that they are not proper to be considered by you against her.

Gilbert paused and scanned the faces of the twelve jurors before continuing:

The statements made by this woman were induced by offers and promises; by surrounding her with imprisonment and isolation, and treating her in such a manner that these statements cannot be considered voluntary. We shall also insist that there was no motive for the commission of this crime. No murder can be committed without a motive. We shall show the effect of her illness upon her body and upon her mind, and it will be left to the jury to decide whether at the time the offense is charged this woman was in such mental condition that she could not be guilty of any crime.[125]

Boyd followed Gilbert and added his two cents. During his remarks, Boyd offered several alternatives to the coldblooded murder Smith envisioned: Mrs. McKnight took strychnine to calm her frayed nerves and gave poison to John Murphy in an attempt to becalm him. Boyd also hinted that Murphy accidentally gave himself an overdose when he said that John Murphy suffered from an addiction to medicine.

Besides, Boyd noted, Mrs. McKnight enjoyed a spotless reputation and lacked a motive for murder. The title to the Murphy property, which Smith held up as the reason for the alleged slayings, was in the name of John's brother James, so even though McKnight raised the mortgage, she could not have obtained the land by foreclosure. Mary McKnight couldn't collect the insurance money, either, since it would likely go to Gladys, the child of John Murphy's first wife. Mary was, Boyd argued, mentally unbalanced by a nervous condition that made her putty in the hands of Sheriff Creighton and E.C. Smith, who coerced her into signing a false confession.

After the lengthy opening statements of Mary's defense attorneys, Chittenden dismissed the jury and adjourned for the day.

"WHEN DOCTORS DISAGREE."

MEDICINE MAN. — There ought to be a law passed to squelch you humbugs!
MENTAL HEALER. — I'm no more a humbug than you are.   Neither of us is infallible; but I do far less harm than you do!

"When Doctors Disagree." Cartoon by artist Louis Dalrymple and published in the April 6, 1898 edition of *Puck*. The dangers of patent medicine are represented by the "Chockfull Cemetery" behind the "Medicine Man." William Chalker later said that Mary "took enough patent medicine to kill a livery stable of horses." Was this a contributing factor in the murders of the Murphy family? *Library of Congress.*

The court did not conduct business on Sundays, so the case resumed on Monday, December 7, 1903.

Boyd and Gilbert would spend most of the morning using defense witnesses to explore Mary McKnight's mental stability.

Margaret Chalker stated that her sister suffered from nervous spells. She described lengthy bouts of despondency during which Mary appeared anxious and blue, as if she carried some unseen burden on her shoulders.

Mrs. Anna Jenson, who employed Mary as a housekeeper and whose daughter, Dorothy, appeared in the newspaper lists of probable poison victims, also testified about Mary's nervous condition. But, she added, these spells never prevented Mary from completing her housekeeping chores.

Boyd called Mrs. Alice Dalzell, a resident of Bay City. Mary stayed at her house while she received treatment from Dr. Stone. Dalzell described Mary's high-strung nature, her periodic panic attacks and a tendency for her mind to wander.

James, Charles and Dan Murphy returned as defense witnesses. Each described Mary's poor health. Traverse City's Dr. Garner went a step further when he testified that Mrs. McKnight's illness periodically caused temporary insanity.

By the end of the afternoon session, Boyd had exhausted his chain of witnesses, and the defense rested.

The morning papers carried headlines about the McKnight trial alongside breaking news of another possible poisoning case near Coldwater along the Indiana border in southern Michigan.

As the McKnight jurors retired for the day on December 7, police arrested Katie Ludwick on suspicion of poisoning her husband, John, with arsenic just ten days after they exchanged vows on November 4, 1903. As the cell door closed on Katie Ludwick in the Branch County jail, a crew led by Deputy Sheriff James Fisk and two Bronson physicians unearthed John Ludwick's body. They removed the stomach, intestines and kidneys and sent them to the chemistry lab at Ann Arbor.

Two weeks earlier, twenty-one-year-old farmer John Ludwick had fallen sick after Katie served him a glass of milk. At first, he believed the milk had spoiled, but then crippling headaches, dizziness and stomach pain landed him in bed for most of Friday, November 20. That evening, Dr. Cornell visited the Ludwicks' house and found the farmer in a bad state. Between the vomiting and the diarrhea, John couldn't keep anything down. Cornell was mystified about the cause of John's ailment but prescribed some medicine for the stomach pains.

John Ludwick's condition went from bad to worse as the night progressed. By Saturday afternoon, he was in too much agony to get out of bed. According to Katie, John told her he was going to die and begged her to fetch his brother. She left the house at 7:30 p.m. and returned an hour later only to find that John had died while she was away. Then, oddly, she left his body in bed while she attended the wedding of a friend.

Neighbors became suspicious. John Ludwick was the picture of perfect health, and the young couple had walked down the aisle amid rumors of an arranged marriage and a very unhappy bride.

Eighteen-year-old Katie Bistry didn't want to marry a man she had seen just four times, but her family arranged the match. Dutifully, she followed their wishes to the altar after a two-week courtship, but neighbors suspected the teenage widow may have found a way out of her vows. They contacted Branch County sheriff David A. Buck, who launched an investigation.

Katie denied buying poison, but the records of Bronson druggist A.J. Ashbreck indicated she purchased arsenic twice on November 17—just three days before John Ludwick died. A clerk at the store insisted he sold Katie ten cents' worth of Paris Green—a toxic substance containing strychnine—and on another occasion, ten cents' worth of arsenic. The clerk also recalled that Mrs. Ludwick said she wanted the poison to kill rats.[126]

On the same morning that Boyd and Gilbert questioned witnesses about Mary McKnight's psyche—December 7—Sheriff Buck received word from Dr. Gomburg in Ann Arbor: John Ludwick's internal organs contained more than twenty-seven grains of arsenic, enough poison to kill a dozen healthy farmers.

Buck arrested Katie and threw her into a cell on the upper story of the county jail in Coldwater. Incredulous, she lay for hours curled into a ball on her cot and stared at the opposite wall, seemingly oblivious to the possibility of a murder charge.

Katie, like Mary McKnight, had become big news. The *Detroit Tribune* sent a reporter to cover the arrest. "The young woman," the *Tribune* correspondent observed, "lies most of the time on her cot in the cell silent and tearless, and hardly seems to comprehend the nature of the awful charge against her."[127]

The *(Coldwater) Courier and Republican* of December 7 ran a front-page article under the title "BRONSON MYSTERY." In an adjacent column was an article about a local man, William Payne, who suffered from ill health. In a fit of "melancholia," the distraught man downed a glass of water spiked with a teaspoonful of Paris Green. Payne's suicide attempt was foiled by his mother, who found him in the nick of time and brought him to a doctor, who pumped his stomach.

At the time, no one recognized any parallels between Payne's suicide attempt and John Ludwick's suspicious death, but local attorney E.E. Palmer read the news with a raised eyebrow.

During the morning session of December 8, Smith called rebuttal witnesses to counter Mary McKnight's insanity defense. Anna Jenson returned to the stand and testified that while she did observe periods in which Mary appeared nervous, she never noticed any signs of emotional instability.

Mrs. Lightheiser followed Mrs. Jenson to the stand. She had attended both funerals: the late April ceremony for Gertrude and Ruth Murphy and the early May wake for John Murphy. Mary, she said, appeared calm and unfazed by the deaths.

Smith recalled Dr. Garner, who earlier testified that Mary's physical condition likely altered her mental state. With a series of caustic questions about Garner's education and experience, the prosecutor successfully eroded the doctor's credibility. By the time Garner left the witness box, he looked like a country sawbones who had no knowledge about mental health or experience in treating mental illness.

Smith's last rebuttal witness was Dr. O.R. Long, a physician for the asylum for the criminally insane in Ionia. Long provided the coup de grace for countering Mary's insanity defense. Answering a hypothetical question, Long explained that a woman of approximately forty-five years of age, undergoing menopause and suffering from depression and anxiety, would not, based on those factors alone, be considered insane. He did not refer to Mary by name, but his inference was clear to everyone in the court. Mary McKnight, according to Long, was sane.

During a sharp cross-examination by Parm Gilbert, Long admitted that a deteriorating physical condition might contribute to mental instability and said he had treated patients with symptoms similar to Mrs. McKnight's. But Long's admission wasn't enough to undo his testimony about Mary's sanity.

Long was the last witness in the case. The morning session ended when he stepped down from the witness box. The jurors shuffled out of the courtroom with Deputies Paquette and Torrey behind them.

The afternoon session was devoted to closing arguments. Attorneys on both sides of the aisle addressed the jury. In his closing comments, which took about an hour, Smith outlined the evidence. He jabbed his finger at Mary McKnight and described her as a criminal of the lowest degree. The prosecutor's condemnation caused Mary to wince, *Detroit Tribune* writer Nathan observed. Smith's scathing comments also "caused her to drop her head still further."[128]

In a three-hour barrage aimed at the emotions of the jurors, Attorneys Boyd and Gilbert offered an alternative explanation for the murders. Their remarks consumed the remainder of the afternoon session and most of the next day's morning session.

When the lawyers finished at about 11:00 a.m. on the morning of December 9, Chittenden turned to the twelve men in the jury box and gave them instructions before they began deliberations. In his final comments, Chittenden addressed the issue on everyone's mind—the lack of a motive:

> *The failure of the people to prove a motive would not be a valid excuse for finding the prisoner not guilty. The law regards all people sane, unless it is shown at the time of the commission of the offense charged the person charged with the crime was of that state of mind that she had no comprehension of right or wrong. If the defense proved beyond all reasonable doubt that the defendant had administered or caused to be administered to the deceased, John Murphy, the strychnine capsule which caused his death, intending him no harm whatever, she was to be acquitted. So far as the death of Mrs. Murphy and babe were concerned, they were admitted into the case only in so far as they might tend to show whether or not the prisoner had guilty knowledge of the effect of the deadly drug which she was administering.*[129]

Chittenden laid out the requirements for a guilty verdict. Mary McKnight must have been proven to be "of sane mind" at the time of the crime, and she must have given poison to John Murphy with the intent to murder him.

12

"They Imitated
Lucretia Borgia"

Wednesday, December 9, 1903

In Big Rapids, Prosecuting Attorney Joseph Barton had reached an impasse in the George Stewart case. A coroner's inquest ruled that Stewart died from strychnine poisoning administered by an unknown person. Barton had just one suspect: Stewart's wife, Emma. She purchased poison on the eve of his death, and a search of the Stewart farmhouse uncovered a package with two grains of poison missing.

But after interviewing neighbors, Barton could find no concrete evidence to implicate Emma Stewart. He held an arrest warrant for her but decided not to issue it.

The case against Emma Stewart died with Barton's decision, but an unexpected development would later revive it.

As a kerosene lantern on a table outside her cell flickered, Caroline Collins's cellmate at the Shiawasseee County jail, an alleged kidnapper named Clarissa Mullins, continued to ramble. "She nearly talked an arm off me," Collins complained to a Detroit reporter. Mullins, who doubled as a self-proclaimed spiritualist, talked incessantly, often channeling the spirits. She said they told her Caroline Collins was innocent.

Unfortunately, the court didn't listen to the spirits; they ordered Collins to stand trial for the alleged murder of George Leachman.

The turnkey blew out the light, which Mullins read as a cue to stop her chattering. With the cell dark and now quiet, Collins contemplated the evidence presented against her during the examination.

"Up to the present time the people have not produced a scintilla of evidence against Mrs. Collins," her attorney, John T. McCurdy, argued. "They must prove Leachman died of acute or slow arsenic poisoning to get any cast against her."

Odell Chapman countered, "There have been swung from the gallows people against whom there was less evidence of murder than against this woman."

Chapman called Sheriff Daniel Gerow, who told the court that during his sweep of the Collinses' residence, he failed to discover any arsenic. Nonetheless, an old army surgeon, Dr. D.H. Lamb, testified that Leachman's symptoms matched those of someone who died from slow arsenic poisoning. Whoever poisoned Leachman, Lamb believed, fed him small doses over a lengthy period of time.

Dr. Jacob Shoemaker, the physician who treated Leachman, testified about the victim's cause of death. He explained that he believed Leachman died of acute pneumonia. Even though slow, methodical poisoning by arsenic could possibly lead to a weakening of the system that could in turn lead to pneumonia, the doctor still believed Leachman died of natural causes. "I think, if pneumonia hadn't set in," he explained, "Leachman would have recovered."[130]

Despite Shoemaker's opinion, the court had heard the word "arsenic."

McCurdy argued that the half grain of arsenic in Leachman's stomach was the result of embalming. He also wanted to provide an alternative possibility in case the court still believed in the prosecution's slow poisoning theory. So he attempted to show that systematically poisoning someone with small doses of arsenic required a detailed knowledge of the drug, and Carrie Collins didn't possess that knowledge. Besides, there was no viable motive for murder, so McCurdy tried to convince the court that George Leachman committed suicide.

The most damning testimony came from Amelia Leachman, the victim's mother. Mrs. Leachman told the court about a strange sight she witnessed while George lingered on his deathbed. She eyed Caroline Collins tiptoeing into the room with a spoon in her hand. When Collins noticed her standing there, she quickly tucked the spoon into a fold of her dress and disappeared into Leachman's room. A few minutes later, her son began to wretch and heave.

Amelia Leachman raised more than a few eyebrows in court when she described another incident that occurred a few days later. She heard a moan coming from George's room and decided to take a look when Carrie Collins appeared and stood between her and the door, blocking her entrance. "It's all right," Collins reassured her, "George is only a little nervous."

An *Evening News* reporter watched Mrs. Collins during the examination. Curiously, she didn't appear fazed. "Through all this gruesome testimony Mrs. Collins, who is alleged to have preferred more than a friendly interest in Leachman during his life, listened with some evidence of weariness," he wrote. "She yawned and acted bored." During a break in testimony, she remarked, "I wonder if I'll get any Christmas present[s] this year?"[131]

The lack of motive didn't hinder the court. In June, Carrie Collins would face a jury for the murder of George Leachman.

She hadn't flinched when she heard the decision. But alone in her cell, in the dark, she began to weep.

After spending a few days behind bars in the Branch County jail, Katie Ludwick opened up to Sheriff Buck's wife, Kittie, and admitted to serving John Ludwick arsenic-laced milk two days before he died.[132] She admitted to purchasing five cents' worth of arsenic and stirring the entire amount into the fatal cup. She later repeated the confession to her father and Father Hewitt, the priest who married the couple.

"I am a Catholic, and under the laws of that church I could not get a divorce," Katie explained on the afternoon of Wednesday, December 9. "My parents compelled me to marry the man and, as I could not live with him, I killed him."[133]

Katie also told Mrs. Buck that she had become smitten with a young acquaintance named George Kosmerick, who promised to marry her as soon as John Ludwick was out of their way. According to Katie, on the day of her wedding to Ludwick, Kosmerick told her, "If you poison John, then I'll marry you."[134] Since Katie couldn't obtain a divorce, she turned to arsenic. Curiously, the portion of Katie's statement that implicated Kosmerick did not make it into the Detroit or Grand Rapids articles about the confession.

Carrying a warrant charging Kosmerick with "inciting to murder," Buck arrested him, brought him to the Branch County jail and dragged him in front of Katie. It was the ultimate he-said, she-said scenario. She repeated the accusation; Kosmerick denied it. Authorities believed Kosmerick and released him.

A *(Coldwater) Courier and Republic* writer called the murder of a husband "the blackest crime known to law." The writer didn't wait for a trial and characterized Katie, the "murderess," as "rather a good looking girl, but is apparently below the mental average. She does not seem to appreciate the seriousness of her crime."[135]

With her confession, the writer admitted, Katie Ludwick saved the county the expense of a trial, but Katie's "crime" wasn't a cut-and-dried affair, as Sheriff Buck would soon realize. The confession, which had evolved from several versions, would become a major controversy in the days ahead, raising accusations of coercion.

Nonetheless, reporters across the state wrote articles about Katie's confession and made their best efforts to link the story to the McKnight trial. Almost the entire front page of the December 9, 1903 edition of the *(Detroit) Evening News* was devoted to news about Michigan's Borgias. A large picture, plucked from the Ludwicks' wedding album, showed the young bride standing next to her husband under the headline "BRIDE OF THREE WEEKS CONFESSES TO MURDERING HER HUSBAND." The caption stated, "She admits killing her husband with poison and shows no remorse for the deed."

In the column adjacent to the photograph was Nathan's latest article about the McKnight trial entitled "MARY M'KNIGHT AWAITS HER FATE." The piece detailed Judge Chittenden's instructions to the jury.

At the center of the page, directly above the pieces about Ludwick and McKnight, the *Evening News* editor strategically placed a political cartoon titled "MICHIGAN'S GREATEST POISONING CASE." The cartoonist used the news of Michigan's Borgias to make a political statement. In an obvious reference to the McKnight and Ludwick cases, a "Political Borgia" wearing an apron and a dress pours a cup of coffee for a farmer seated at the kitchen table. The coffee represents "POLITICAL STRENGTH AND POWER FOR THE DEAR FARMERS," but behind her back, the Borgia holds a bottle of poison labeled "BOSS RULE."[136]

The news of Michigan's Borgias traveled across the country. A *(New York) Sun* writer observed, "Death from poisoning would seem to be epidemic in Michigan just now."[137] Seizing on the theme first introduced by a Detroit journalist, the *Minneapolis Journal* ran a front-page article under the headline "THEY IMITATED LUCRETIA [*sic*] BORGIA."[138] The article outlined the cases of McKnight, Collins, Ludwick and Stewart.

13

Verdict

CADILLAC, MICHIGAN

Thursday, December 10, 1903

The jury remained deeply divided about Mrs. McKnight's guilt. Bothered by her lack of motive, five jurors wanted acquittal. After a few hours of discussion, two of them changed their votes to guilty. The last three jurors held out for the rest of the morning.

Mary McKnight anxiously awaited their decision with her sister. Margaret Chalker, apparently convinced of Mary's guilt, supposedly confronted her. "This will probably be our last moments alone," she said as she held Mary's hand. "They will probably send you to prison for life. Now I want to know why you killed them."

"I have nothing to say," McKnight replied.[139]

About noon, word leaked from the courthouse that the jury had reached a decision. Mary McKnight, flanked by her sister Margaret Chalker and Margaret's husband, William, entered the courtroom, which was standing-room only when Judge Chittenden called for the jurors. "Her face was expressionless, but her steps feeble," wrote the *Grand Rapids Herald* reporter who made the sixty-mile trek north from the Furniture City to Cadillac.[140]

After deliberating for twenty-eight hours, the jury returned its verdict at about 1:30 p.m. on the afternoon of December 10, 1903. The gallery listened in silence as the foreman, Henry Gilbert, stood and read the verdict:

guilty as charged. All eyes turned to Mrs. McKnight. "Motionless she sat," the *Herald* reporter said as Chittenden noted that "he could not see, in the light of the evidence presented, how any intelligent jury could have brought in any other verdict."[141]

Smith requested immediate sentencing. Judge Chittenden turned to McKnight and asked her to stand. William Chalker took a hold of her arm and gently tugged, pulling her onto her feet. When Chittenden asked if she had any objection to his passing sentence, McKnight muttered, "I did not mean them any harm."

A view of a cellblock in the Detroit House of Corrections, circa 1880, from a stereo view card published by L. Black and Company in Detroit. *Author's collection.*

Chittenden addressed the prisoner. "You have been found guilty of the crime of murder and what makes it worse is that the victim is your brother. In pronouncing sentence on you I have no choice in the matter, but had I the power to lighten the sentence I should have to give you the full extent of the law. Mrs. McKnight, the sentence of this court is that you spend the remainder of your natural life in the state's prison at Jackson."[142]

A wide range of emotions filled the courtroom. While McKnight appeared stoic, Smith and co-counsel Totten received congratulations. Overcome with emotion, Sheriff Creighton slumped back into a seat, cupped his face in his hands and wept.

Residents of Alpena, where Mary was suspected of poisoning her first husband and her second husband's first wife, followed the case closely through their local paper. "The sentence gives unusual satisfaction," wrote the *Alpena Evening News* correspondent.[143]

The next morning, December 11, 1903, Mary said goodbye to the Chalkers at the train depot. Margaret hugged Mary and promised to write. William said he would look after Mary's affairs and visit her after the New Year.

A *Detroit Tribune* photographer seized the opportunity and snapped a photograph of McKnight with her veil raised, which the *Tribune* writer noted was rare because "even while in the courtroom she had remained heavily veiled, shutting out all view from the curiously inclined and has furthermore kept her head bowed at all times."

The photograph, the reporter said, illustrated the physical change in the defendant. "Before her arrest she weighed no less than 160 pounds. The slight figure depicted in the photo will now scarcely tip the scales at 126." The caption appeared under the title "MRS. MCKNIGHT, THE MURDERESS."[144]

A portion of the death certificate showing cause of death for John Murphy with the addendum, "Murdered—strychnine poisoning." A similar statement was added to the death certificates of Ruth and Gertrude Murphy. *Michigan Department of Community Health.*

After Mary's farewell to the Chalkers, Sheriff Huckleberry escorted her south to Jackson, where he would deliver her to A. Vincent, warden of the Michigan State Prison. After processing, she would be rerouted to the Detroit House of Corrections, Michigan's primary facility for female inmates. The sheriff allowed Mary to have the window seat so she could view, one last time, the Michigan countryside as the train sped past verdant fields and pastures.

Back home in Kalkaska, the county coroner thumbed through the death records. He plucked three out of the file cabinet and placed them side by side on his desk. He turned toward the death certificate of Isaiah John Murphy, dipped his fountain pen and added three words in the section under cause of death. He then added the same three words to the death certificates of Gertrude Murphy and Ruth Murphy: "murdered—strychnine poisoning."[145]

Part 4

Epilogue

The Fates of the Players

While Mary spent her first six months in jail, the other women dubbed "Michigan Borgias" by the press went to court for their alleged crimes.

The trial of Caroline Collins wrapped up in early June, about a week before Katie Ludwick would face a jury in Coldwater.

Parker and his co-chair Odell Chapman based their case on the theory that the defendant had slowly poisoned Leachman to get rid of him so she could marry Colonel Northwood.

Testimony consumed almost four weeks. Parker called a series of doctors to show that Leachman died from poisoning and another series to show Collins's alleged motive for the deed. The prosecution also questioned witnesses about the death of Ira Wright, for the purpose of proving three points: the intent to kill, the presence of arsenic in the Collins home and the likelihood that Caroline Collins understood the drug's deadly effect.

Calm, cool and collected, Caroline Collins took the stand in her own defense and withstood a scathing attempt to prove that she and hired hand Leachman were lovers. She insisted that their relationship was purely platonic and hinted that the rumors were started by a servant she had dismissed for incompetence.

By the end of the fourth week, Collins's counsel, John T. McCurdy, felt good about his chances of an acquittal. Prosecution witnesses, he believed, had failed to prove that George Leachman died of poisoning—a possibility noted by Judge Smith when he instructed the jury. If the evidence, Judge Smith said, indicated that Leachman died of pneumonia, and the arsenic

The Detroit House
of Corrections, circa
1900. Women serving
long-term sentences did
their time at this facility.
*Detroit Publishing Company,
Library of Congress.*

in his system resulted from the embalming process, they must vote for an acquittal. Unless, Smith warned the twelve men, the evidence proved beyond all doubt that George Leachman ingested arsenic before he died, they could not find Carrie Collins guilty as charged. He also instructed them to consider Ira Wright in their deliberations only as evidence that Collins possessed arsenic and then only if they believed the arsenic found in the boy's system was not the result of embalming.

The jury deliberated for about three hours. Carrie Collins stood, shocked, as she listened to the foreman of the jury pronounce her guilty of murdering George Leachman. The verdict stunned Collins's friends and neighbors, who followed the testimony and expected a favorable outcome. Colonel Northwood was heartbroken; he planned to marry the widow if she was acquitted.

Carrie Collins kept a stiff upper lip in court, but back in her cell, she broke down and blamed malicious gossips for her ordeal. A newspaperman eavesdropped on the emotional scene, jotting her every word in a notebook: "If I were guilty I could stand this, but before God I am innocent. This will kill mother. Spite work and money have brought this upon me."[146]

Three weeks later, Judge Smith sentenced Caroline Collins to a life of hard labor in Jackson. While Collins traveled south to Jackson, the county coroner changed George Leachman's death certificate. His handwritten annotation reflected the uncertainty some felt about the guilty verdict. He wrote "[murdered by arsenic?]" as the "immediate cause of death."[147]

The trial, based primarily on circumstantial evidence, was the most expensive in Shiawassee County. It cost taxpayers a whopping $14,000.

Carrie Collins followed Mary McKnight's footsteps to Detroit. From Corunna, Sheriff Gerow and his wife escorted the widow to Jackson. After processing, she was transferred to the Detroit House of Corrections.

A reporter for the *(Owosso) Evening Argus* described her as "in appearance...anything but a typical murderess. She is...plump, brown-eyed, and of a decidedly motherly appearance."[148] She was shy, quiet and a model prisoner. At the House of Corrections, Prison Superintendent McDonnell put her to work in the carding department.

If she got to know Mary McKnight in Detroit, their relationship was short-lived. A life sentence for Caroline Collins lasted just under two years.

While Collins settled into her cell, John T. McCurdy appealed her case to the Michigan Supreme Court. After examining the trial transcript, Justice Ostrander became convinced that George Leachman wasn't poisoned but instead died of pneumonia, as Dr. Shoemaker had testified. Although

Ostrander couldn't convince all his fellow justices about Leachman's cause of death, five of them agreed that certain aspects of the case warranted a new trial. They based their decision in part on the judge's decision to allow certain testimony regarding the death of Ira Wright, which they found to be prejudicial.[149] "I hope for a different verdict the next time," Carrie Collins said when she heard the good news.[150]

Collins was discharged from the Detroit House of Corrections on May 26, 1906, and sent back to the Shiawassee County jail, where she awaited her retrial. Her time in E.T. Barnum's cage was limited to just three months. In mid-August, Judge Miner ordered her released on $5,000 bail.

A few days later, a group led by A. Adams, a wealthy farmer and longtime friend of Caroline Collins, raised her bail money. Colonel Northwood was not one of them. During Collins's stint in prison, he married another woman.

On August 22, Adams arrived at the county jail in his carriage to bring the prisoner home. As he flicked the reins and the horses sped away, Caroline Collins looked back at the stone edifice and smiled. She was free at last.

She would not return. Shiawassee County officials decided not to pursue the case against her.

Katie Ludwick's trial got underway in mid-June. In many ways, her trial was a mirror image of Mary McKnight's. Like Mary, Katie denied the confession she allegedly made to Kittie Buck, so any hope of a quick, clean conclusion to the sordid case ended with her examination on December 30, when Justice White found sufficient reason to conduct a trial.

Because the newspapers carried items about Katie's confession, the attorneys went through dozens of prospective jurors in their efforts to empanel a jury. The men finally selected became virtual prisoners, with Deputy Sheriff Knauss escorting them to and from the Hotel Arlington "as a kindergarten teacher might [lead] her class of infants out for a picnic and none were allowed out of his sight."[151]

Witnesses testified in front of a standing-room-only crowd made up of mostly women, "drawn by the novelty of seeing a woman tried for murder."[152]

Katie's confession became the focal point of the trial. Sheriff Buck, Mrs. Buck, her sister and Deputy Sheriff James Fisk all testified about the various admissions the suspect made about dosing her husband with arsenic. In the first version, Kittie Buck said, Katie admitted buying arsenic at her husband's request. She stirred the arsenic in coffee, which her husband carried to the barn. Katie said she didn't see him drink it.

Mrs. Buck didn't believe her and asked her to tell the truth, so Katie revised her story.

In a later version, given to both Mrs. Buck and her sister, Katie said she mixed the arsenic with milk and watched her husband down it. Sheriff Buck and Deputy Sheriff Fisk testified that Katie told them she had given Ludwick two doses and burned the rest, and in a later version, Buck said, she admitted to serving Ludwick poison on three occasions. Regardless of these variations, the witnesses said, Katie admitted to poisoning either her husband's coffee or milk.[153]

Dr. Baldwin testified about an experiment he conducted. He stirred 120 grains of arsenic into a glass of milk and found that 100 grains of it either dissolved or remained suspended in the fluid, and the poison didn't alter the flavor. He replicated the experiment with coffee and found similar results. Baldwin's experiment proved that Katie could have easily slipped twenty-seven grains or more into her husband's drink undetected.

Katie's own words, it seemed, would damn her to a life sentence, but then her defense attorneys began their case. They recalled Sheriff David Buck and his wife and grilled them about coercing Katie's alleged confession.

Through a series of defense witnesses, attorney E.E. Palmer created reasonable doubt by depicting John Ludwick as a depressed farmer who asked his wife to acquire arsenic and mix it in milk to make a rat trap when in fact he had suicide on his mind. John Ludwick, he argued, used the same suicide method Coldwater resident William Payne did, only with arsenic instead of Paris Green.

Palmer reminded the jury about Katie's original statement, in which she said she prepared the arsenic-laced coffee at her husband's request. He reminded them about Kittie Buck's refusal to accept this explanation, implying that the sheriff's wife needled the frightened girl into an incriminating—and false—admission. He pointed out that Katie Ludwick's primary language was Polish, thus raising the possibility that something had been lost in translation. The crafty attorney also summoned three scientists from Detroit who countered the prosecution's forensic evidence.

By the end of the trial, the defense attorneys had so completely shattered the prosecution's case that it took the jury just twelve minutes to return a verdict of "not guilty." Rather than deride Katie Ludwick for getting away with murder, the courtgoers who watched the drama congratulated her and celebrated the verdict.

"Never, probably," wrote the *(Coldwater) Courier and Republican* reporter sent to cover the trial, "has a prisoner accused of the crime of murder had the sympathy of a community more than has Katie Ludwick. At first they believed her guilty, but as the prosecution's case unraveled in court and her attorneys tore it to shreds, the sympathy of a large proportion of the citizens of Coldwater went over to the fair prisoner."[154]

In mid-April, a neighbor of Emma Stewart sent a letter to Governor Aaron T. Bliss demanding an investigation into George Stewart's cause of death. After consulting with Joseph Barton, the governor was satisfied that Barton made the right decision in not arresting Emma Stewart.

A few months later, on June 24, a group of neighbors sent a signed petition demanding action. This time, Bliss opened a full investigation into the crime and Barton's conduct in the case. Deputy auditor general Henry E. Chase and Bliss's secretary, Herbert E. Johnson, arrived in Big Rapids on August 24 and interviewed all of the major characters in the story.

As Chase and Johnson collected evidence, the *Detroit Free Press* ran an article under the headline "Old Case Is Revived." According to the *Free Press* reporter, there was talk that Bliss's investigation into the prosecutor's conduct was engineered by Barton's political enemies. They wanted to smear Barton's reputation as he geared up to run for a second term.[155]

On September 1, Barton received a letter from Bliss. Dated August 31, the letter applauded Barton and said the prosecutor "acted in good faith and honestly endeavored to perform his official duty in the matter." Bliss went on to explain that he would not interfere with Barton's judgment "as to whether or not a criminal case should be prosecuted."[156]

The governor's letter ended the case against Emma Stewart before it began.

Except for a few disgruntled neighbors, people of the county felt good about Barton's decision. The *Big Rapids Pioneer* heralded Barton's restraint and praised him for keeping the county out of an unnecessary, costly and "more or less hopeless poisoning trial."

The writer did not fail to recognize similarities with the McKnight case:

> *In Kalkaska county a case similar to this came up about the same time as [the] Stuard [sic] case, and is still fresh in the memory of many readers. This is none other than the McKnight case, in which a woman was accused*

of poisoning. The prosecution dragged on for many weary months. Much unsavory testimony was rehearsed, and the end seemed doubtful. At last the verdict of guilty was given, but the trial had cost the county $3,700. This was buying justice at a big price, yet it was worth it if the convicted person was really guilty.[157]

The McKnight trial, it appeared, had an unexpected cost as well. Of the four women labeled "Borgias" by the press, three were innocent victims, their cases almost certainly influenced by the one who was found guilty.

"This is the time of year," griped a *Kalkaska Leader* writer, "when the average supervisor gets more than his share of cussing owing to the prevailing high taxes, all along the line, while as a matter of fact he has very little to do with it."[158]

One of the culprits, the journalist noted, was Mary McKnight. With her case concluded, the county faced the daunting task of paying for it. Smith's experts were particularly expensive. Professor A.M. Clover charged the county $525.00 for his chemical analysis and E.D. Reed, $950.00. Samuel Bell, M.D., charged $276.85 for his expert opinion, and O.R. Long, MD, charged $265.26.

William Wilson's time was comparatively cheap. The Fife Lake undertaker billed the county two dollars.

Wexford County charged $1,460.48 for the use of its courtroom.[159]

Mary was in prison for life, but the story didn't end with her guilty verdict. The murder of John Murphy led to an ugly battle over his estate that pulled his brothers, Dan, Charles and James, into a court battle with Gladys Murphy and her guardian. The case went to court three years later in December 1906.

Once again, Ernest C. Smith and Joshua Boyd would square off in court. Smith represented Gladys Murphy, John's daughter by his first wife. The prosecutor first became acquainted with the question of Gladys's paternity during the McKnight case. After John's death, Mary made inquiries about his life insurance, which sparked off a debate about the deceased's true heir.

With John gone, Gladys stood as the sole heir to her father's forty acres of land in Springfield Township. Her guardian, Daniel C. Hutchins, alleged that John, just before his divorce, deeded the land to his brother James to avoid including it in a settlement with his ex-wife. Just after the divorce became final, Hutchins believed, James returned the deed to John. There was lack of a paper trail, however, because the deed returning the property from James to John Murphy was lost and never recorded.

Three years earlier, Boyd had used this fact—that James Murphy held the only official deed to John's tract of land—in his attempt to discredit Smith's theory about Mary's motive for murdering her brother. The land legally belonged to James Murphy, who planned to pay the money his brother owed to Mary. It wouldn't have made any sense for her to murder John to obtain land he didn't legally own.

Now, Hutchins wanted James to sign the land over to Gladys. Boyd represented James Murphy, who claimed that he, and not John Murphy, owned the property.

The trial became a morass of deception with the various witnesses contradicting one another. James's wife, Jennie, admitted there was no deed but said her husband and John agreed to a contract: James bought the property for $250 with the understanding that after ten years, John would buy it back. Since her husband wasn't home at the time, Jennie signed the contract with two witnesses, although both men didn't actually read the document and couldn't verify its contents.

It was the testimony of one witness, Mrs. Lightheiser, that became the fulcrum on which probate judge William W. Whipple balanced all other statements. The wife of a neighboring farmer, Mrs. Lightheiser helped the Murphy family oversee the property after John Murphy's death.

Mrs. Lightheiser testified about a conversation she said she had with James's wife, Jennie.

Smith questioned the witness. "What, if anything, was said to you by Jennie Murphy at that time relative to the title to the John Murphy farm?"

Boyd stood up. "To that we object as incompetent, irrelevant, and immaterial. Anything that may have been said, if there was anything said, by Mrs. Jennie Murphy, would in no way bind the defendant James Murphy."

Whipple overruled Boyd.

"Yes, sir; there was," Mrs. Lightheiser answered Smith's question.

"What was it?"

"Do you want me to go straight through?" Lightheiser asked.

"Just tell what Mrs. Jennie Murphy said relative to who owned the John Murphy farm."

"The John Murphy property?"

"Yes."

> *Well, she asked me who I thought John Murphy's property would go to, and I told her to Gladys Murphy, and she said: "Well, they will have to prove that there is a Gladys Murphy first." And I says, "Well, Jennie, you people will have to prove that there hain't a Gladys Murphy, or the property will surely go to her." Then Jennie says: "Well, I don't know if she will get anything or not. When John and Clara had their trouble John deeded his place to Jim, and when we deeded it back to John we didn't deed it before any witnesses, and I don't know whether she will get anything or not." "Well," I says, "if any one has anything against the place to hold it, why, it is all right, but, if they hain't, it will go to Gladys Murphy." Then she said, "Well, there is nobody has anything against the place but Mary McKnight. She has a mortgage of $200."[160] "Well," I said, "of course they can take that out, and the balance will go to Gladys Murphy." And I says, "That was only a scheme to keep Clara Murphy from getting what really belonged to her. John just deeded it so as not to let her have any of it."[161]*

Of all the witnesses, Whipple believed Mrs. Lightheiser and credited her testimony as the key evidence in the case.[162] He found for Gladys. Once again, Ernest Smith had bested Joshua Boyd in court.

Boyd immediately appealed the decision. Michigan's Supreme Court scrutinized the trial transcript.[163] Given the importance Whipple attributed to Mrs. Lightheiser's statements, the judges examined them very carefully. They concluded that, while perhaps true, Lightheiser's testimony did not establish the existence of a deed from James to John Murphy. The court reversed Whipple's decision, effectively disinheriting Gladys.

As the Murphy family squabbled over John's forty acres and Kalkaska residents "cussed" at the Michigan Borgia for causing their taxes to spike, Mary settled into her cell in Detroit. The State Prison of Southern Michigan at Jackson wasn't typically used to house female inmates, so after being

The Detroit House of Corrections, circa 1900. Note the armed guard on the roof. The penitentiary held some infamous females, including outlaw legend Belle Starr and the "Michigan Borgia," Mary McKnight. *Detroit Publishing Company, Library of Congress.*

processed, Mary was sent to the Detroit House of Corrections, where she spent the majority of her time behind bars.[164]

The Detroit penitentiary had a colorful history. When the prison opened in 1861, it became Michigan's primary facility for female inmates. Over the years, some notorious characters did time there, including the infamous outlaw Belle Starr, a federal prisoner who spent eighteen months in Detroit for horse theft.[165]

Life behind bars wasn't all bad for Mary McKnight. She was forced away from patent medicine, and her mind became clear. She also went from picking at her plate to eating full meals again. Almost immediately, she regained seven pounds.[166] Shortly after arriving in Detroit, she went to work in the prison's button department.

From behind the barred windows of her cell, Mary watched as the midsized city grew into a sprawling metropolis thanks in large part to Henry Ford's assembly line and promise of a five-dollar wage for an eight-hour shift.

Robinson	Mary	Inmate	F	W	57	Wd
Barnett	Elizabeth	Inmate	F	W	40	M1
Burlingame	Bertha	Inmate	F	W	26	M1
Underwood	Ada	Inmate	F	W	49	M1
Bouchard	Clara	Inmate	F	W	49	M1
Quimby	Sarah	Inmate	F	W	40	Wd
...man	Neva	Inmate	F	W	21	M4
Oehlerkehin	Pearl	Inmate	F	W	24	S
Williams	Beulah	Inmate	F	W	21	M1
Fleming	Madge	Inmate	F	W	21	S
Pope	Nellie	Inmate	F	W	50	Wd
Pauli	Lida	Inmate	F	W	35	M1
Flood	Jennie	Inmate	F	W	47	Wd
Larsen	Mabel	Inmate	F	W	34	M1
Jones	Lillian	Inmate	F	B	27	S
Ferguson	Ida	Inmate	F	Mu	28	M1
McCoy	Mamie	Inmate	F	W	38	M1
King	Emma	Inmate	F	W	34	M1
Rehm	Dora	Inmate	F	W	39	D
Cummings	Louise	Inmate	F	W	25	M1
Johnson	Rachel	Inmate	F	B	56	M2
Smith	Maud	Inmate	F	Mu	33	M1
Reynolds	Eliza	Inmate	F	Mu	59	D
Lewis	Elma	Inmate	F	W	19	M1
Russell	Gertrude	Inmate	F	W	46	Wd
Noода	Frances	Inmate	F	W	3-	
McKnight	Mary	Inmate	F	W	55	Wd
Model	Emma	Inmate	F	Mu	26	M1
Trauss	Nehlmina	Inmate	F	W	68	Wd
Landau	Eliza	Inmate	F	W	61	Wd
Conklin	Belle	Inmate	F	W	39	M1
Hubbard	Della	Inmate	F	W	36	Wd
May	Frances	Inmate	F	W	42	Wd
Schapn	Kittie	Inmate	F	W	36	M1
George	Anna	Inmate	F	W	47	M2
Bowers	Mary	Inmate	F	W	28	S
McKee	Hattie	Inmate	F	Mu	27	M1

Three excerpts from the 1910 federal census represent a roster of the thirty-seven Michigan women housed in the Detroit House of Corrections. *National Archives.*

On a bright, brisk morning in mid-February 1904—two months after Mary's trial ended—William Chalker visited his sister-in-law in Detroit. As her power of attorney, he made the trek from Grayling to discuss her remaining assets and a possible appeal of her sentence.

Chalker didn't know what to expect as a guard led him down a cathedral-like corridor containing three tiers of cells. The guard ushered Chalker to the button department, where Mary was sitting at a table, sewing buttons onto clothes. He was pleasantly surprised by the rotund figure sitting on the bunk.

When she noticed Chalker enter the room, she became very emotional. Her lips quivered and tears streamed down her cheeks. Chalker told a *Detroit Journal* correspondent:

I noticed at once the change for the better. At Kalkaska, she couldn't recognize me, her mind was in such a bad state. But now it is clear and normal.[167] *Her appearance has greatly changed. She is fatter and healthier. She has been eating a rational amount of food and it has had a beneficial effect. She used to be a very sickly woman and took enough patent medicine to kill a livery stable of horses. The doctors used to tell her she would never be well until she was operated on.*

"She seems quite contented," Chalker paused and realized how no one could feel "contented" in a prison cell. "That is, as much as possible. Of course, she expressed a desire for her freedom. But she said that she was well treated at the house of correction, and the matrons told me that my sister in law was a model prisoner. She never gives any trouble, although they expected it and dreaded her coming." He continued:

> She is getting more religious than she used to be, although she was always an attendant at church. But now her mind has turned in that direction more than ever and when I spoke about her condition and her hope of freedom, she said: "I place my trust in God. He is the only one who can help me now." As for the new trial, I can't tell whether we will endeavor to secure one or not. Mrs. McKnight said she would leave the matter entirely with me.

A Kalkaska reporter used the Chalker interview to do a follow-up piece on the county's most infamous woman, although she wasn't front-page fodder anymore. The story appeared on the back page of the *Kalkaska Leader*. "Mrs. Mary McKnight, the Kalkaska Borgia…is growing fat and religious," the reporter summarized Chalker's statement. "She has cast aside her patent medicines, declares that she is now putting her trust in God and the result has been a decided change for the better both mentally and physically."[168]

The prison's high walls could not keep news from filtering in from the streets of Detroit, and from this prison pipeline, Mary learned about the horseless carriage, the Wright brothers' flying contraption and other technological marvels of the twentieth century.

It was on a frigid day in late March 1916 when she first heard about the poison plot of Arthur Warren Waite. A dentist from Grand Rapids, Waite attempted to acquire his wife's family fortune by poisoning his in-laws one by one.

The prize that Arthur Warren Waite eyed was the seven-figure fortune of Grand Rapids pharmacy baron John Peck. After marrying Peck's daughter, Clara, Waite hatched a plan to inherit his father-in-law's nearly limitless wealth. He successfully poisoned John Peck's wife, Hannah Peck, in the fall of 1916 and, just a few weeks later, finished off John with a dose of arsenic in his bowl of soup. Once Clara inherited her half of the Peck fortune, Waite planned to do away with his plain-Jane wife to make room for his true love, married cabaret singer Margaret Horton. His master plan went awry when friends and relatives became suspicious. An investigation uncovered the plot, and Waite went to trial.

Like Mary, Waite tried an insanity plea, but his beloved Margaret turned state's evidence and testified against him. She destroyed his insanity defense

Hannah Peck, the first victim of convicted poisoner Arthur Warren Waite. *Bain News Service, Library of Congress.*

when she read a letter Waite penned from prison. After a period of time in a mental institution, Waite promised, he would whisk her away to a life of leisure.

It became evident to the jury that Waite wanted to finance his playboy lifestyle with the Peck fortune. His get-rich-quick scam landed him on Sing Sing's death row. He took the long walk to the electric chair on May 24, 1917.

Arthur Warren Waite, whose plot captivated the nation's headlines for months, became one of the most notorious figures in Michigan's history.

Arthur Warren Waite poses for a photograph during a break in his 1916 trial for the murder of his in-laws. *Bain News Service, Library of Congress.*

Mary McKnight, who was once characterized as engineering "one of the most horrible crimes that has ever stained the annals of Michigan," was no longer the criminal cause célèbre of Michigan poisoners.[169]

While Mary stitched buttons, the Murphy family passed several milestones. Dan Murphy married Hattie Hilton in South Boardman in 1908, and James Murphy and his wife, Jennie, celebrated the birth of their fourth child in 1911. A year later, seventeen-year-old Gladys married a Kalkaska farmer named Forrest Wheeler. Although the Supreme Court ruled against her in the land dispute, Gladys did inherit a portion of John Murphy's estate. Probate court documents indicate that Daniel Hutchins held a sum of money in trust until Gladys turned twenty-one.

In April 1920, the family mourned two losses within two weeks. Mary's power of attorney and advocate, William Chalker, died in April 3, 1920. Nine days later, James Murphy died on April 12, 1920.

Mary McKnight had served eighteen years of her life sentence when the parole board decided to release the sixty-seven-year-old. Just before noon on June 19, 1920, the door to her cell at the Detroit House of Corrections gave a metallic shriek as it swung open.[170] A news correspondent described her: "In spite of her long imprisonment and hard work the years have dealt kindly with her. Her abundant hair is still coal black with only an occasional gleam of silver about the temples, her brown eyes are clear and her figure is erect."

The correspondent watched as McKnight said farewell to her best friend, Mary, a seventy-four-year-old woman who was seven years into a life sentence. The two women embraced each other. After a few seconds, somewhat reluctantly, Mary let go. With tears rolling down her cheeks, she pressed a handkerchief into McKnight's hand. She wiped away the tears with her shirt sleeve and managed a slight smile.

"I know I'm going to miss Mary dreadfully at first," McKnight remarked as a guard led her and the correspondent through the prison block. They could hear Mary's sobs as they made their way to the office.

A clerk handed her $4.16, the amount of money she brought when she was transferred from Jackson State Penitentiary except for the $0.50 she spent to have her glasses fixed. The clerk then handed her a roll of banknotes totaling $290.50, which represented the interest that had accrued during her eighteen years behind bars. During her time inside, Mary had been thrifty, spending only a few pennies here and there on sundries like fruit.

She emerged from the building at high noon. Robert and Susan Ogg, Detroiters whom she had befriended, were waiting to take her to their home.

Susan was on the board of directors for the Michigan Training School for Women and had agreed to house Mary during her period of parole.[171]

Mary shuddered as an automobile motored past. She watched as the car—a blue Cadillac Roadster—sped down Russell. It was clear that a lot had changed.

As Mary McKnight passed time in her cell, Detroit had grown from a small midwestern city into one of the nation's largest metropolises. The same year she went to prison—1903—the Ford Motor Company was founded. In 1911, Henry Ford offered five dollars for an eight-hour-shift, which brought thousands to his factories. Detroit became the Motor City and eclipsed the one-million-citizen mark around 1920.

"I came here in a horse cab," Mary remarked, "but after all I've been through I guess I shouldn't be afraid of this, should I?" She held on to the correspondent's hand as she climbed into the back seat of Ogg's car.

"You see," she continued, "once I visited in Alpena before I came here and I saw two or three automobiles then, but they made so much noise that they scared me almost to death. I suppose they're quieter now, aren't they?"

As Ogg pulled away from the prison, Mary looked back at her home for the last eighteen years. "There's the kitchen," she noted, "and there's the dining room, and the girls won't be seeing me there any more."

After a brief stop at the bank, Robert Ogg drove Mary McKnight through Detroit to his home. She marveled at the rows of houses. "These little houses make me think of home. I almost can think I'm going back there again."

Mary stared out the window as she absorbed the sights of urban Detroit.

"Do you always have so many cars out or does it just happen so? It makes me dizzy to see them," she mused as the correspondent jotted her words into his notebook. "And it seems so queer to be going so far away. You see, for almost 16 years I never had my feet on the ground. Not till last summer when the new board came in were we allowed to go out in the yard. We could see out of the windows, but never in all that time could I stoop down and smell a posy growing."

She turned her head as they motored past a house with a flower box containing geraniums in full bloom. The palette of colors reminded Mary of her first husband, James Ambrose, the painter.

"And on Saturday night we were always locked in our cells and could not get out until Monday morning," she continued as she looked out the window. Now we got out in the yard Sunday afternoon, after we go to church, and it did seem so good," she said.

The sun was shining so brightly, Mary used her hand to shield her eyes and continued:

The first two years I was here we didn't have any lights at all in our cells. And it was terrible to be shut up at night in the pitch darkness. And we had to work so hard. Why, my job every day for the longest while was to sew on buttons, and I had to sew twenty gross of them a day. When the days were short we had to sew in the dark, and it was all I could do to do my stint. I've always worked hard, and often I've made 20 pairs of trousers a day.

"How did you feel when you learned of your release?" the reporter asked.

"How did I feel when they told me I was going to get out? Well, they told me late yesterday afternoon, and said they'd arrange it that night if I really wanted to. But I told them I guessed one night more wouldn't hurt me any. Only I couldn't somehow get to sleep. Every few minutes I'd open my eyes to see if the light was breaking and as soon as it did I dressed and I've been ready ever since."

A few minutes later, they arrived at the Ogg residence. Tears formed at the corners of Mary's eyes when Susie Ogg showed her the bedroom that was to be hers. "How'll I ever learn to sleep in a real bed again? It's been nothing but that hard, narrow cot so long."[172]

Mary returned to the living room. She sat down on the edge of a chair and rubbed her hands together as if she didn't know what to do with them.

"Can't I show you something?" Mary asked the reporter. She pointed to the two small boxes on the floor by the foot of her chair. "It's my crocheting."

She reached into one of the boxes, pulled out some bolts of cloth, and set them on her lap. "It's my crocheting, you see. For 27 years, I hadn't touched a crochet hook, for it wasn't until Dr. Mary Thompson Stevens came on the board last summer that we women were allowed to have any kind of fancy work, and for a few years before I came here, I hadn't had time for crocheting. But I can't tell you what it has meant to me and to the other women to have something for pick up work when we get to our cells at night."

She patted the cloth on her lap and smiled. "They told me that crochet cotton was going up in price so I got a chance to buy these two boxes, and I did. I had to give up buying any fruit for two weeks to do it but I thought it was worth it. They let us buy fruit, but we can draw only so much money, you see, and I let the fruit go."[173]

Mary McKnight died a few years after her release from the Detroit House of Corrections. Although details of her interment are unknown, one thing is certain: she was not interred in the family plot at the Springfield Cemetery.

⊷⊶⊜ ⊜⊶⊷

Charles Murphy, who never married, lived on a farm in Springfield Township for the rest of his life. He died of a heart attack in 1947. He was interred in the Murphy family plot next to his sister Sarah at the Springfield Cemetery.

Daniel Murphy lived most of his life on a Springfield Township farm alongside his second wife, Etta. He died in 1950 at the age of seventy-seven and was also buried in the family plot, next to his brother Charlie and sister Sarah at the Springfield Cemetery.

Margaret (Murphy) Chalker died in Grayling on January 2, 1930, at the age of sixty-nine. Martha (Murphy) Woodard died in Fife Lake on October 2, 1937, at the age of seventy-four.

Seventeen-year-old Gladys Murphy married nineteen-year-old Kalkaska farmer Forest Wheeler on December 13, 1912. Together, the couple had five children: twins who died in infancy and three daughters. Gladys (Murphy) Wheeler died in 1983 at the age of eighty-seven.

After the completion of his second term in 1904, Sheriff John W. Creighton purchased a local livery and ran the business until automobiles made livery barns obsolete. He died in 1932 at the age of sixty-nine.

In 1908, Clyde C. Chittenden left Michigan and moved west. He settled in Seattle, Washington, where he continued his career as a successful entrepreneur as the owner and president of the Edgewater Mill Company. His company cleared much of the land that later became the northwest side of the city. He also invested in real estate with his other business, the Chittenden Land Company. He died in 1953 at the age of ninety-two.[174]

Ernest C. Smith served as Kalkaska's prosecuting attorney for several years after the McKnight trial. He left the office in 1922 and became the assistant attorney general to Andrew Dougherty, but after successfully prosecuting several cases, he resigned to pursue private practice from his new home in Petoskey. He died in Emmet, Michigan, on April 15, 1966, at the age of ninety-two.

Joshua Boyd continued to practice law in Kalkaska County. In 1922, he began his second stint as the county's prosecuting attorney when he replaced Ernest C. Smith. He served throughout the turbulent Roaring Twenties. He died on April 9, 1935, in Muskegon at the age of seventy-eight.

Parmius C. Gilbert went on to a long and celebrated career as prosecuting attorney for Grand Traverse County. Perhaps motivated by his experience with the McKnight case, he became a champion of prison reform, advocating for a system in which first-time offenders went to a camp rather than to a prison, where older, more experienced convicts could bully and browbeat them. In 1929, he won a position as circuit court judge and served until illness forced him to step down from the bench in 1945. He died on April 30, 1950.[175]

15
There's Something about Mary

There are two great unknowns in the McKnight case. The first, a natural question regarding alleged serial killers, involves her true number of victims. Intent aside, she poisoned three people—Ruth, Gertrude and John Murphy—and a close examination of the case suggests there may have been several others. Just about every newspaper with a journalist covering the McKnight case ran a list of eleven alleged victims. Although records are sketchy and the evidence is circumstantial at best, there is some indication Mary may have murdered a few of the people on this list.

Whereas the symptoms of arsenic poisoning—diarrhea and vomiting—appear frequently in other illnesses, the convulsions and back-bending that occur when strychnine cripples the central nervous system are uncommon. In other words, there are hundreds of maladies that may cause a person to lose control of his bowels, but comparatively few cause a person to lose control of his nervous system.

Several alleged victims of Mary McKnight suffered from convulsions, fits or spasms before they died, and their death records provide a chronicle of doctors baffled by seemingly healthy people suddenly keeling over and dying for no apparent reason.

The death record of Dorothy Jenson—one of nearly a dozen on Mary's alleged hit list—provides a good example. The doctor who signed her death certificate wrote, "Don't know" under the immediate cause of death. For duration of the illness, he wrote "15 min.?" Baffled, he wrote that the Jenson girl died from "over-exertion" after "skipping rope." Since he didn't witness the girl's death, he relied on statements made by the last person to see her alive, which was customary for the era. And that person was Mary McKnight.

Ditto Ruth Murphy. Ditto Gertrude Murphy. Ditto John Murphy.

Mary, apparently, made no attempt to fabricate cover stories, since the death records illustrate just how puzzled the doctors were in some of the cases. Ruth Murphy died after unexplained "spasms," Gertrude died following an "epileptic fit" and John died after his asthma triggered a massive seizure. If Mary intentionally murdered them, she never intended to hide behind phantom symptoms.

Family members either wittingly or unwittingly obscured the truth about John Murphy's death. They told Dr. Pearsall that John suffered from debilitating bouts of asthma and believed it contributed to his death. Perhaps they did believe this, but in retrospect, it seems like they were grasping at straws, or worse, attempting to cover up some wrongdoing. There was some bad blood between Dan and John over John's first wife; perhaps they wanted to keep Dan's name out of the headlines. Or perhaps they believed John committed suicide and wanted to keep it a secret locked in the family closet (especially if John's life insurance contained a clause that nullified the policy in case of suicide).

There could have been others whom Mary eyed as potential patients. In the late '70s, a Murphy descendant told author Larry Wakefield that Aunt Mary wanted to give James Murphy's son, James Ray, some medicine in the form of a white powder. James wouldn't allow it, and the boy survived.[176]

The second unknown in this case involves motive.

Sometime during her early years, Mary McKnight acquired some experience in nursing or midwifery. Among her friends and intimates, she might have become a valuable medical resource in an area where doctors were few and far between. In any case, she positioned herself as caregiver to Ruth, Gertrude and John Murphy and probably many others. As such, Mary McKnight joins other felonious caregivers in a category of criminal sometimes referred to as an "angel of mercy" or an "angel of death."

This type of criminal uses her position as caregiver to harm rather than heal for various reasons that can range from financial gain to a sadistic joy of killing.

Theory One

Mary Murdered for Money, or the "Mercenary Motive"

Ernest C. Smith championed the "mercenary motive" and based his entire case on it. As evidence, he turned to the mortgage document, which Mary first brought to the register of deeds only days after John's death. With John and his beneficiaries out of the way, the forty acres would go to John's creditor, Mary McKnight, or his next of kin, his mother, Sarah. In either case, the prosecutor reasoned, Mary would control the land since she ran the Murphy household for her aged mother. Mary also made overtures about obtaining her brother's $1,000 insurance policy, which brought Gladys Murphy into the picture.

Gladys Murphy's claim to her father's land also destroyed the idea that Mary would gain indirect control of John's land when it passed to Sarah Murphy. Under cross-examination by Parm Gilbert, Smith begrudgingly admitted that he represented Gladys in the probate battle, thus undermining his own theory of the crime. As for the insurance policy, the $1,000 hardly seemed motivation for a woman who came to Springfield Township with $4,000 that she collected from policies on her two deceased husbands.

No one in Judge Chittenden's court, it appeared, bought Smith's theory. The scant references to the trial in the surviving news accounts hint that the prosecution failed in its attempt to prove any viable motive for the murder of John Murphy. In fact, Smith's case fell so flat in this regard that Judge Chittenden found it necessary to advise the twelve men on the jury that they didn't need motive to return a guilty verdict.

Theory Two

Mary Loved Funerals

Reportedly a belief of some Murphy descendants, this theory suggests that Mary murdered because she loved attending funerals.[177] A traditional Irish funeral is a multilayered affair involving a keening and two funerals. Relatives come from near and far to mourn and then celebrate the life of the dearly departed. As a female kinswoman, Mary would have played a seminal role in the wake of a close relative. Perhaps, with no immediate family of her own, she felt a desperate need to belong and found a way to satisfy her cravings by manufacturing funerals with poison.

It seems a bit far-fetched, given the fragility of life in the northern Michigan wilderness, that Mary would need to engineer funerals. Premature death caused by disease or accident was a part of early twentieth-century life. It was the ideal world for a death junkie.

If on the other hand, Mary was that into black taffeta and lace, then she apparently had an insatiable lust for it. Her brother Willie died just months before Ruth, Gertrude and John.

THEORY THREE

Malignant Hero

One "angel of mercy"–style killer is the malignant hero, a caregiver who manufactures illness because she craves the attention she receives from ailing patients. When she "saves" her patient, she becomes the hero.

Yet the typical malignant hero attempts to save patients. There is no evidence that Mary attempted to save either Ruth or Gertrude and thus had very little interest in becoming the "hero" in those cases. There is a slight chance she might have tried to save John, although the massive amount of poison Dr. Reed discovered in John's stomach suggests she had no intention of even attempting to appear at the eleventh hour as her brother's savior.

THEORY FOUR

Sadist with a God Complex

Another type of "angel of mercy" thrives on the power she possesses over people who fall under her care; she loves to play God and sometimes kills because she takes great pleasure in taking lives. There is typically a sadistic angle to these types of crimes.

In her alleged confession, Mary insisted she wanted to help, not harm, John Murphy. For a person who claimed to want to soothe people, Mary made a curious choice of drugs. While an overdose of strychnine kills quickly, it hardly produces a pain-free death. She could have purchased any number of drugs—opium, morphine, heroin, cocaine, laudanum—that would have done a much better job of killing a person's pain permanently.

It would have been easy enough to obtain potentially lethal drugs, such as paregoric (a potent cocktail of opium and alcohol), from the corner pharmacy. These substances were less controlled than alcohol, which was considered the greater of two evils. One of the cases immediately preceding the McKnight trial in Cadillac involved a local barkeep named Peter Anderson who violated the town's blue laws when he sold liquor on Sunday from his saloon at 209 South Mitchell Street. The charge noted that Anderson was "not being then and there a druggist."[178] In other words, while a saloonkeeper couldn't sell on the Sabbath, a pharmacist could legally sell any number of substances on Sunday without violating official ordinances.

If Mary wanted to poison her relatives in a pain-free manner that would have not left the tell-tale clue of convulsions, all she needed to do was visit a pharmacy, but instead, Mary chose a deadly poison that left her victim's bodies in knots.

As she was a person with some rudimentary medical training and a self-proclaimed user of strychnine, it seems likely that Mary would have known how much was too much. If Mary knew that she gave her brother an overdose and understood the deadly results, then it could be argued that she wanted him to suffer.

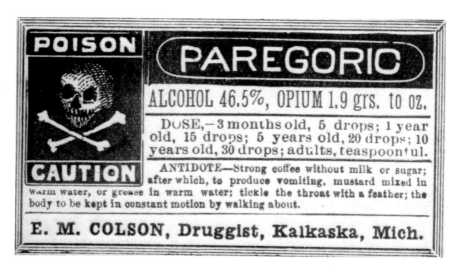

Drug label for paregoric sold by a Kalkaska druggist, circa 1900. The drug was a potent combination of alcohol and opium. Note dosages for children. *Author's collection.*

"The Age of Drugs." This cartoon, drawn by Louis Dalrymple and published in the October 10, 1900 edition of *Puck* magazine, makes a satirical statement about the availability of intoxicating substances. The saloonkeeper, represented by the man smoking

a cigar, can't compete with the proprietor of "Killem Quick Pharmacy," open "all night." Note the little girl holding a bottle of "soothing syrup." Such medicines, marketed for use by children, often contained opium. *Library of Congress*.

Then again, maybe Mary chose strychnine because she could obtain it without raising any suspicions. In 1903, people purchased poison every day to kill rodents. Battenfield wouldn't have questioned why she wanted five cents' worth of strychnine.

THEORY FIVE

Mary Never Intended to Harm Them

According to this theory, Mary was innocent, at least of any malice. She was, as she said, just trying to help. As incredible as it sounds, this may be the best explanation for Mary McKnight's motives.

While she admitted giving poison to Ruth, Gertrude and John Murphy, she insisted she never intended to hurt them. Gilbert and Boyd plied the jury with an alternative scenario: Mary mistakenly gave Ruth medicine from the wrong package and consequently gave Gertrude and John some of her medicine, which contained strychnine, to help them cope.

During the trial, this explanation understandably fell short of explaining John's death. The forensic evidence didn't support it; the sheer amount of poison in John Murphy's stomach proved he ingested far more than a few tablets. This scenario also ran counter to logic—a point quickly recognized by Ernest C. Smith. After accidentally poisoning Gertrude Murphy, Smith argued, Mary would not make the same mistake twice. Surely Mary, with her background in medicine and her own use of the substance, would know the drug's lethality. This idea made an accidental poisoning of John Murphy appear an impossible-to-believe scenario.

Perhaps the real mistake, however, was in assuming Mary made a mistake in giving her victims overdoses of strychnine. Instead, maybe she intended to poison them because in her altered sense of reality, she was helping them.

The key to Mary's mental state may lie deep in her past at a critical time when, as a young mother, she lost not just one child, but all five. Little is known about Mary's life with her first husband, James Ambrose. Having grown up with eight siblings, perhaps Mary dreamt of a large family. After their first three children died in infancy, the couple finally had two beautiful daughters who survived. Tragically, neither Minnie nor May Ambrose lived to see the age of five.

It's not hard to imagine the scenario from this point forward.

The grief sends Mary into a deep depression that worsens as she watches the families of her siblings grow. James and Jennie have four children; Margaret and William Chalker, three; Martha and Jerome Woodard, two; and John and Gertrude, one.

Meanwhile, Mary begins a lifelong struggle with anxiety and depression. She discovers the soothing effects of strychnine in small doses and perhaps in attending to an injured neighbor, she takes a nip of paregoric or laudanum and begins a long-term addiction to one or more substances.

The depression coupled with her substance use skews her perception. She accidentally gives Ruth Murphy strychnine and the baby dies. Gertrude is inconsolable with grief. Mary doesn't want the poor woman to experience the long-term grief she knew all too well from losing five children, so in her altered sense of reality, she heals Gertrude by poisoning her. Gertrude's death seals John's fate, as once again, Mary turns to strychnine to soothe her brother's pain. This makes her what a twenty-first-century criminologist might call a mercy killer.

The descriptions of Mary's demeanor provide some clues to a possible substance abuse problem. At trial, Creighton said Mary constantly rattled the bars of her cage, suggesting she was gripped by withdrawal; in her confession, she spoke of her brother's ghost visiting her, hinting at possible hallucinations; and after Boyd visited her in the Kalkaska County jail to discuss her alleged confession, he said, "She has no recollection of having made any statement." He also characterized her as not "mentally responsible."[179] Conversely, when William Chalker saw her in the Detroit House of Corrections eight months later, when steel bars forced her away from the bottle, he described her as possessing a lucidity she lacked while in the Kalkaska lockup.

Chalker's statement following his Detroit visit is telling. Mary, he said, "used to be a very sickly woman and took enough patent medicine to kill a livery stable of horses."[180]

THEORY SIX

Aunt Mary, with a Vengeance

Theory six suggests a more sinister corollary. Deprived of her own family, depressed and hooked on patent medicine cure-alls, Aunt Mary becomes a felonious home wrecker. She uses her drug of choice—strychnine—to make sure others feel the pain she experienced after losing her children.

Consulting the Murphy family tree, it becomes apparent that Aunt Mary is linked with the deaths of at least one child in each of her sibling's families up until her incarceration in 1903. She may have made an attempt on James Ray (James's eldest child), she was suspected in Eliza Chalker's death (Margaret's eldest child) and she admitted poisoning Ruth (John's daughter). This theory would also explain the deaths of other unrelated children, such as baby Teeple and Dorothy Jenson, who appear on the list of Mary's potential victims.

Theory Seven

Mary the Sociopath

Armchair detectives often lump convicted murderers into the category of "sociopath." There isn't enough known about Mary's personal life to categorize her as a sociopath, and what little emerges from the court documents and news reports suggest that she doesn't appear to fit the profile.

The prototypical sociopath lacks remorse and will often make prolonged eye contact that is sometimes described as icy and emotionless. While in the Kalkaska jail, Mary told Ernest Smith about John Murphy's ghost forgiving her, which suggests she acknowledged the need for forgiveness and felt a certain degree of remorse.

Further, almost every reporter who attended the trial described Mary as shielding her face with a black veil and dropping her head to avoid eye contact, hardly the actions of a remorseless person.

Sociopaths also typically lie with the best of them and are expert manipulators, but Mary wasn't very good at either, even when she tried. She stumbled for an explanation about the presence of strychnine in the Murphy home, repeatedly changing her story to fit the known facts. At first, she said the only poison in the home was some strychnine she mixed with cornmeal and put in the cellar for rats the previous winter. When Creighton and Smith discovered she purchased poison from a Fife Lake druggist just days before John Murphy's death, she changed her tune. She said that this was the poison she put in the cellar, thus exposing her earlier story as a deception. Clearly, she was not an adept liar with years of practice.

Regardless of what motor moved Mary, if she went to trial today, she likely would have wound up in an institution, where psychiatrists would probe the dark corners of her psyche. Even in 1903, when illnesses of the mind were little understood, there was speculation about Mary's mental faculties. Despite Smith's effective line of rebuttal witnesses countering her insanity defense, the jurors had their doubts. According to some sources, they deliberated twenty-eight hours because several jurors, convinced Mary was insane, held out.[181]

According to William Chalker, there was something about Mary that left others scratching their heads. "The doctors used to tell her," Chalker said, "she would never be well until she was operated on."[182]

Timeline

April 20, 1903	Gertrude and Ruth Murphy die in Springfield Township.
May 2, 1903	Isaiah "John" Murphy dies in Springfield Township.
May 31, 1903	Mary McKnight arrested at Walton Junction.
June 8–9, 1903	Mary McKnight allegedly confesses to murder.
October 23, 1903	George Leachman dies in Hazelton Township.
November 14, 1903	John Ludwick dies in Bronson Township.
November 30, 1903	Emma Stewart purchases strychnine in Big Rapids; Mary McKnight arrives in Cadillac.
December 1, 1903	McKnight trial begins in Cadillac (ends December 9); George Stewart dies on a farm five miles from Big Rapids.
December 7, 1903	Katie Ludwick arrested on suspicion of murder.
December 8, 1903	Examination of Caroline Collins begins in Corunna; Katie Ludwick allegedly confesses to murder; a coroner's jury finds that George Stewart died of strychnine poisoning.
December 10, 1903	Jury finds Mary McKnight guilty of murder.

December 11, 1903	Big Rapids prosecuting attorney finds insufficient evidence to indict Emma Stewart for the murder of her husband.
December 30, 1903	Examination of Katie Ludwick begins in Coldwater.
May 10, 1904.	Collins trial begins in Corunna (ends June 8).
June 8, 1904	Jury finds Caroline Collins guilty of murder.
June 13, 1904	Ludwick trial begins in Coldwater (ends June 28).
June 28, 1904	Jury finds Katie Ludwick innocent of murder.
September 1, 1904	Upon reviewing evidence in the case, Michigan governor A.T. Bliss supports the decision of Big Rapids prosecuting attorney Joseph Barton not to prosecute Emma Stewart for the murder of George Stewart.
May 26, 1906	Caroline Collins released from the Detroit House of Corrections after the Michigan Supreme Court orders a new trial.
August 22, 1906	Collins leaves the Shiawassee County jail on parole pending a new trial. Shortly after, the county decides to drop the case.
June 19, 1920	Mary McKnight released on parole.

Notes

INTRODUCTION

1. Today, the cemetery is known as Springfield Township's Clark Cemetery, but it has been known by various names throughout the years. Because contemporary accounts of the case (court records and news articles) refer to it as the Springfield Cemetery, that is the name used throughout this text.

CHAPTER 1

2. Sources differ concerning Gertrude Murphy's age. Her tombstone indicates that she died at age twenty-two, while her death certificate lists an age of nineteen. The federal census of 1900 gives a birth date of 1883, making her nineteen years old in April 1903.
3. Brower, who ran a grocery store in Fife Lake, also served as undertaker. Fife Lake is just across the Kalkaska County line from Springfield Township.
4. According to the official death certificates, Ruth died about 2:00 p.m. and Gertrude about 3:00 p.m.
5. Michigan Department of State, certificate and record of death of Gertrude Murphy; certificate and record of death of Ruth Murphy. Death records from this era are available on microfilm at the Michigan Department of Community Health, on microfilm at the Library of Michigan or online at *Seeking Michigan*. The originals are held by the counties.

6. *Grayling Avalanche*, December 4, 1902; Michigan Department of State, certificate and record of death of William Murphy.
7. An itemized bill indicates that the embalming was done by Willis Brower, but court documents indicate that twenty-three-year-old Fife Lake resident William L. Wilson worked on the bodies. It is possible that Brower employed Wilson to help him with the undertaking portion of his business. Interestingly, found among Brower's things was a bottle of Concentrated Frigid Jr., a product of Chicago's Frigid Fluid Company designed for use in the embalming of children.

Chapter 2

8. Direct examination of Joseph B. Battenfield, *The People of the State of Michigan v. Mary McKnight*.
9. Ibid. The quotes attributed to both Battenfield and John Murphy come from Battenfield's testimony at Mary McKnight's examination.
10. In the first phase of a traditional Irish wake, the body is washed, clothed and placed in a bed.
11. Michigan Department of State, certificate and record of death of Isaiah John Murphy.
12. Direct examination of Joseph B. Battenfield, *The People of the State of Michigan v. Mary McKnight*. The quarantine suggests lingering doubts about Murphy's cause of death.

Chapter 3

13. According to some sources, Mary McKnight gave Gertrude a footbath to comfort her. Strychnine poisoning can occur following an external application.
14. Powers and Cutler, *History*, 135.
15. *Hutchins v. Murphy*, 623. Ownership of the land was uncertain and became the focus of another trial in 1906. During testimony in *Hutchins v. Murphy*, Dan Murphy testified that he brought the mortgage to the county registrar for recording. He asked who owned the property, and when the registrar of deeds told him that his brother James held the deed, Dan replied, "Just as I expected, he [John] didn't have no deed on record." The mortgage document was brought to Kellogg after John's death, and Smith

used this fact as evidence that Mary murdered John to gain control of his land. But technically, James Murphy owned the property. Dan Murphy's testimony suggests that the family was aware of this fact.

16. *Biographical History*, 521–22

17. Direct examination of Ernest C. Smith, *The People of the State of Michigan v. Mary McKnight,* June 25, 1903.

18. John Murphy may have had an ulterior motive for not filing this altered mortgage document. He may have wanted the courts to believe his brother James owned the land. See chapter 14, "The Fates of the Players."

19. Ibid.

20. The *(Traverse City) Evening Record* delicately described the divorce in the June 3, 1903 edition: "The reasons alleged were statutory, Dan, the brother, being implicated, and the paternity of the child, born five months after the divorce, being disowned by John."

21. John and Clara reapplied for a marriage license in August 1896, indicating that they tried to reconcile, but they never remarried and ultimately decided to split up for good.

CHAPTER 4

22. Some sources place the exhumation as early as May 18, but this is an error. According to most accounts, including contemporary stories in the *(Traverse City) Evening Record*, Mary traveled to Traverse City to find legal counsel to block the exhumation and was arrested on May 31 on her return trip. If John Murphy's body was exhumed almost two weeks earlier from the Springfield Cemetery, not far from the Murphy farm, Mary Murphy would certainly have known about it and would not have needed help in preventing what had already occurred. Various news accounts also place the exhumation during the week prior to Mary's arrest.

23. *Biographical History*, 523–25; Direct examination of Dr. Perly W. Pearsall, *The People of the State of Michigan v. Mary McKnight,* June 25, 1903, 10–13.

24. Direct examination of Dr. Perly W. Pearsall, *People of the State of Michigan v. Mary McKnight,* June 25, 1903, 10–13. Dr. Pearsall's testimony indicates that he examined the body and removed the stomach at the cemetery and not at a funeral parlor or undertaking establishment.

25. *Biographical History*, 370–72.

CHAPTER 5

26. *Biographical History*, 525–26.
27. Direct examination of Daniel Murphy, *The People of the State of Michigan v. Mary McKnight*, June 25, 1903.
28. Cross-examination of Ernest C. Smith, *The People of the State of Michigan v. Mary McKnight*, June 25, 1903. Other than Mary McKnight, Smith was the only person present during this exchange, which Smith recollected under oath during the preliminary examination. The treatment of the prisoner remained a controversial topic throughout Mary McKnight's trial. Mary's defense attorneys alleged that Smith's kindness was a strategy to lure her into making incriminating statements.
29. *(Traverse City) Evening Record*, June 4, 1903.

CHAPTER 6

30. U.S. Census 1870, family of Isaiah Murphy; U.S. Census 1870, Mary Murphy in Household of William and Sophronia Leach. In the federal census of 1870, Mary Murphy is not listed as a member of the Isaiah Murphy household, which indicates that she left home sometime at or around the age of fourteen. Her father and brothers worked in the lumber industry during the winter months, so it is likely Mary also left home to help the family make ends meet on the farm.
31. Michigan Department of State, certificate and record of death of Ja. Ernest McKnight.
32. Ibid., certificate and record of death of Dorothy Jenson.
33. *Detroit News Tribune*, June 5, 1903. This article is the earliest instance in which Mary McKnight is characterized as a Michigan Borgia. This nickname would be repeated by journalists throughout the United States.
34. *(Traverse City) Evening Record*, June 5, 1903.
35. Ibid., June 6, 1903.
36. *(Detroit) Evening News*, June 6, 1903.
37. Ibid.
38. Ibid., June 13, 1903.
39. Quoted in *(Traverse City) Evening Record*, June 8, 1903. Smith was mistaken when he referred to Gertrude Murphy as a "girl of 29 years"; Gertrude was twenty-two when she died. See note 2.

CHAPTER 7

40. Quoted in the *Grand Rapids Post*, June 11, 1903; *(Traverse City) Evening Record*, June 11, 1903. The *Grand Rapids Post* contained only two portions of the alleged confession; the *Evening Record* printed the entire statement. No official record of the alleged confession has survived. The statement, allegedly signed by Mary McKnight, was admitted into evidence during the trial, but the trial record no longer exists.

41. Cross-examination of Ernest C. Smith, *The People of the State of Michigan v. Mary McKnight*, June 25, 1903, 21–39. According to some news sources, Smith received Reed's telegram on June 11, but during his testimony at the preliminary examination, Smith said he received this note on June 9.

42. Cross-examination of Ernest C. Smith, *The People of the State of Michigan v. Mary McKnight*, June 25, 1903, 21–39.

43. Mary's alleged confession appeared in the *Grand Rapids Post*, June 11, 1903; *(Traverse City) Evening Record*, June 11, 1903; *Detroit Tribune*, June 11, 1903; *Alpena Evening News*, June 11, 1903; and others.

CHAPTER 8

44. Quoted in *(Traverse City) Evening Record*, June 11, 1903.

45. *Detroit Free Press*, June 11, 1903.

46. *(Traverse City) Evening Record*, June 11, 1903.

47. *Detroit Tribune*, June 11, 1903.

48. Ibid.

49. *Alpena Evening News*, June 11, 1903.

50. *Toledo (Ohio) Sunday Bee*, June 11, 1903.

51. *New York Times*, June 11, 1903.

52. *(Detroit) Evening News*, June 13, 1903. Janette goes on to describe the view from Mary's cell: "Looking through barred windows, on one side [is] a railroad half buried in sand, on the other side revealing a landscape of tamarack scrub with a naked, sandy hill looming up in the horizon in the far distance."

53. Ibid. The Kalkaska Historical museum contains a prison cell from the early part of the twentieth century that could have conceivably held the county's most infamous prisoner.

54. *(Detroit) Evening News*, June 13, 1903.

55. Ibid.

56. *Alpena Evening News*, June 12, 1903.

57. Ibid.

58. *Detroit News Tribune*, June 13, 1903.

59. The front-page article about the McKnight case in the June 11, 1903 *(Traverse City) Evening Record* included a list in three parts: "Murders confessed," "Possibly poisoned" and "Other deaths." Grand Rapids and Detroit newspapers from the same date included similar lists.

60. Boyd's first explanation appears to be an act of desperation, but it is an interesting comment about the degree of sensationalism sometimes created by the era's media. While few reporters of 1903 stooped to fabricating quotes, they did sometimes present information in a misleading manner. For example, see Katie Ludwick's confession.

61. *(Detroit) Evening News*, June 13, 1903.

62. Ibid.

63. *(Traverse City, MI) Evening Record*, June 16, 1903.

64. Ibid., June 17, 1903.

65. Ibid.

66. *(Detroit) Evening News*, June 16, 1903.

67. Ibid., December 3, 1903.

68. Cross-examination of Ernest C. Smith, *People of the State of Michigan v. Mary McKnight*, June 25, 1903, 21–39. Smith's wording here is inaccurate. The arraignment took place on June 10. Mary asked for a postponement of her examination or preliminary hearing. In his testimony, Smith identifies the reporter as "a Detroit Journal man."

CHAPTER 9

69. *(Traverse City) Evening Record*, June 26, 1903.

70. The trial transcript is in question-and-answer format. It is presented here as dialogue to create a more readable narrative. Attribution tags have been added, but the wording of the testimony remains unaltered.

71. Direct examination of Joseph G. Battenfield, *The People of the State of Michigan v. Mary McKnight*, June 25, 1903, 1–7.

72. Cross-examination of Joseph G. Battenfield, *The People of the State of Michigan v. Mary McKnight*, June 25, 1903, 7–10

73. Prolonged rigor mortis is a telltale clue of strychnine poisoning. Cold temperatures may also lead to prolonged rigor mortis, and Kalkaska experienced a cold spring in 1903.

74. Direct examination of Dr. Perly W. Pearsall, *The People of the State of Michigan v. Mary McKnight*, June 25, 1903, 10–13.
75. Cross-examination of Dr. Perly W. Pearsall, *The People of the State of Michigan v. Mary McKnight*, June 25, 1903, 13–15.
76. Smith's recollection of McKnight's alleged confession is the only existing official record of the statement. The statement scripted by Smith and signed by Mary McKnight is not part of the trial record. The only extant copies of this statement are those published in newspapers of the era and based on the copy drafted by Smith.
77. Direct examination of Ernest C. Smith, *The People of the State of Michigan v. Mary McKnight*, June 25, 1903, 15–21.
78. Cross-examination of Ernest C. Smith, *The People of the State of Michigan v. Mary McKnight*, June 25, 1903, 15–21.
79. Ibid.
80. Ibid.
81. Ibid.
82. According to a news story in the December 4, 1903 edition of the *(Traverse City) Record Eagle*, Mary McKnight confessed in the presence of others: "Prosecutor Smith secured a confession from the defendant in the presence of the sheriff, and at another time in the presence of Sarah Murphy, her mother, now deceased." Smith's testimony here, however, indicates that no one else was present at the time. This is a good example of the sometimes distorted and sensationalized news coverage of the case.
83. Examination of Dan Murphy, *The People of the State of Michigan v. Mary McKnight*, June 25, 1903, 40–42.
84. Affidavit of Parm C. Gilbert, *The People of the State of Michigan v. Mary McKnight*, September 1, 1903; affidavit of Jacob Tinklepaugh, August 25, 1903; affidavit of Jacob C. Gray, August 25, 1903. In his affidavit, McKnight's attorney Parm C. Gilbert stated that among the newspapers that circulated in Kalkaska, one came from Rapid City, two from the village of Kalkaska (the *Kalkaska Leader* and the *Kalkaskian*) and one from Fife Lake (*Fife Lake Monitor*). In the village of Kalkaska, he noted, newspapers from Detroit and Grand Rapids "were circulating and read in large numbers." At Gilbert's request, both the publisher of the *Kalkaska Leader* and the publisher of the *Kalkaskian* submitted affidavits describing the circulation of their respective papers: 700 copies per week for the *Kalkaskian* and 350 copies per week for the *Kalkaska Leader*.
85. Affidavit of Parm C. Gilbert, *The People of the State of Michigan v. Mary McKnight*, September 1, 1903.

86. Ibid.

87. *Grand Rapids Post,* June 11, 1903.

88. Michigan Department of State, certificate and record of death of Sarah Murphy. "Bilious colic" referred to extreme stomach pain, most likely caused by a liver or gallbladder ailment.

89. Motion by J.L. Boyd and Parm C. Gilbert, *The People of the State of Michigan v. Mary McKnight,* August 10, 1903. They cite three factors in their request to postpone the trial: (1) Mary's ill health, (2) the passing of her mother and (3) the inability of certain witnesses to attend the proceedings.

90. Affidavit of J.L. Boyd, *The People of the State of Michigan v. Mary McKnight,* August 10, 1903. Boyd characterizes Stone as so vital "that she [Mary McKnight] cannot proceed to trial without the attendance of said witness"

91. Ibid. Jenson, Dalzell and Stone all testified at the trial, but there is no record of Dr. Burton's testimony.

92. Ibid.

93. Ibid.

94. News reports and court documents refer to him as "George Leachman," but according to the 1900 census and his death record, his surname was "Lechman."

95. Michigan Department of State, certificate and record of death of George Lechman.

96. Ibid., certificate and Record of death of Ira Nicholas Wright. The timing of the Collins case—the allegations occurring in the fall of 1903—raises the possibility that news coverage of the McKnight case triggered fears of a similar situation in Hazelton and influenced the manner in which authorities handled the case.

97. Ibid., certificate and record of death of Ida May Weisenberger.

98. *Detroit Free Press,* December 1, 1903.

99. *Corunna Journal,* November 19, 1903.

100. Ibid.

101. Michigan Department of State, certificate and record of death of George Stewart.

102. The timing here is interesting. George Stewart died at 9:00 a.m. on the morning of December 1, just about the time when the morning session of the McKnight trial began. The McKnight trial was big news across the state; it is therefore conceivable that news of the McKnight case influenced Mecosta County officials to open an investigation in the death of Stewart.

Chapter 10

103. There is no trial transcript. The court records contain a transcript of the preliminary examination but not of the trial, which is not unusual. Michigan criminal courts, by law, must keep transcripts for a period of only twenty-five years. Records from trials predating microfilm were often discarded, their only remnants preserved in the stories of reporters sent to cover the proceedings. The extant court record, which consists of typed documents on very thin, almost transparent paper, is inside a sleeve marked "Circuit Court for the County of Kalkaska," which is itself inside an outer folder marked "Circuit Court for the County of Wexford."

104. *Detroit Tribune*, December 1, 1903.

105. Ibid.

106. *Grand Rapids Herald*, December 1, 1903.

107. *(Detroit) Evening News*, December 1, 1903 .

108. Wheeler, *History*, 325–27.

109. Wilson likely used Durfee's Embalming Fluid, which was manufactured by the Durfee Embalming Fluid Company of Grand Rapids, Michigan.

110. Sources differ on who proposed the morbid experiment. Some accounts have Reed making the request, while others (*Traverse City Daily Eagle*, December 3, 1903) have University of Michigan chemistry professor A.M. Clover presenting the court with a vial containing poison taken from John Murphy's liver and kidneys.

111. *Grand Rapids Herald*, December 2, 1903.

112. Ibid.

113. *Detroit Tribune*, December 9, 1903.

114. Ibid., December 10, 1903.

115. Holstege, *Criminal Poisoning*, 159. Based on these numbers, John Murphy's stomach contained between twenty-five to fifty times the amount typically taken in medicine and almost twice a lethal dose of half a grain. One sixtieth of a grain is equal to just over a milligram, and half a grain is equivalent to thirty-two milligrams. According to most sources, thirty milligrams is considered a dangerous dose, but the lethal limit varies depending on the individual and can be as little as five milligrams.

116. This testimony suggests that John Murphy suffered from panic attacks. News articles detailing testimony from the Murphy brothers do not state what type of medicine John Murphy allegedly took to alleviate his condition, but at the time, strychnine in small doses was sometimes taken as a mild stimulant. Thus, it is possible that John Murphy took a

medicinal dose of strychnine on a regular basis, although suspiciously, Sheriff Creighton did not find any such medicine belonging to John Murphy when he searched the house.

117. *Traverse City Daily Eagle*, December 3, 1903.

118. Ibid.

119. Ibid.

120. *Detroit Tribune*, December 4, 1903.

121. *Grand Rapids Herald*, December 4, 1903.

122. Ibid., December 5, 1903. The December 4, 1903 edition of *(Detroit) Evening News* printed a slightly different version of this statement: "John will not live two weeks; this grief will kill him."

123. *(Detroit) Evening News*, December 4, 1903.

124. *Grand Rapids Herald*, December 5, 1903.

CHAPTER 11

125. *(Detroit) Evening News*, December 5, 1903.

126. *(Coldwater) Courier and Republican*, June 20, 1904. A study of the Ludwick case reveals the following timeline: on Tuesday, November 17, Katie Ludwick purchased arsenic from Bronson druggist; on Thursday, November 19, she fed it to her husband; John Ludwick died on Saturday, November 21. Another Ashbreck clerk, Glen Keyes, later testified that he sold Katie Ludwick an additional three ounces of arsenic.

127. *Detroit Tribune*, December 9, 1903.

128. Ibid., December 10, 1903.

129. Ibid.

CHAPTER 12

130. *People v. Caroline Collins*, 123.

131. *(Detroit) Evening News*, December 8, 1903.

132. Judge Chittenden sequestered the McKnight jury with the strict instructions that jury members may read newspapers as long as the articles didn't reference the McKnight trial. The Katie Ludwick case made headlines across the state, and most of the articles did not refer to the McKnight case, so it is possible the McKnight jury knew about her confession as it deliberated. While it is impossible to ascertain the impact,

if any, this might have had on the verdict, it raises provocative questions about jury bias. It is also interesting to note that the McKnight trial and the examination of Caroline Collins occurred almost simultaneously (the Collins examination took place on December 8), so it is conceivable that news of the McKnight case might also have impacted the Collins case.

133. *Grand Rapids Herald*, December 10, 1903. Curiously, the primary newspaper in Coldwater, the triweekly *Courier and Republican*, did not contain a quote from Katie Ludwick's confession, while the Grand Rapids newspaper did. Most of the news accounts describe her as "a Polish girl," hinting at possible xenophobia in the community.

134. *(Coldwater) Courier and Republican*, June 24, 1904. During the trial coverage of the case, Mrs. Buck testified about Katie's various statements. According to the sheriff's wife, Katie said she didn't like Ludwick; she liked Kosmerick. A Coldwater news correspondent characterized the relationship in his coverage of the trial. The reporter's word choice hints that the star-crossed lovers didn't wait for the formality of a wedding. "She [Katie] said she liked a man named Kosmerick and had been with him."

135. Ibid., December 9, 1903.

136. *(Detroit) Evening News*, December 9, 1903.

137. *(New York) Sun*, December 9, 1903.

138. *Minneapolis Journal*, December 9, 1903. The *Big Rapids Pioneer* ran a parallel article in its December 10, 1903 issue.

Chapter 13

139. This is an unverified statement printed in the *Grand Rapids Herald*'s coverage of the case on December 11, 1903.

140. *Grand Rapids Herald*, December 11, 1903.

141. Ibid.

142. Ibid.

143. *Alpena Evening News*, December 11, 1903.

144. *Detroit News Tribune*, December 11, 1903.

145. Michigan Department of State, certificate and record of death of Isaiah John Murphy; certificate and record of death of Gertrude Murphy; certificate and record of the death of Ruth Murphy. The alteration of the official death certificates is interesting when considering Judge Chittenden's instructions to the jury regarding Gertrude and Ruth Murphy.

CHAPTER 14

146. *Detroit Free Press,* June 8, 1904.

147. Michigan Department of State, certificate and record of death of George Lechman.

148. *(Owosso) Evening Argus,* May 26, 1906.

149. *People v. Caroline Collins,* 128.

150. *Detroit Free Press,* May 26, 1906. According to her prison record housed in the Burton Historical Library at the Detroit Public Library, Carrie Collins was transferred from Jackson on June 27, 1903, and discharged on May 26, 1906. During her two-year stint, she lost eleven pounds.

151. *(Coldwater) Courier and Republic,* June 15, 1904.

152. Ibid.

153. The *Courier and Republic* journalist sent to cover the case noted that the court employed an interpreter because "a number of the Polish witnesses are unable to speak English." Katie Bistry was a first-generation American, born in Michigan, but it is likely that her primary language was Polish. This raises the interesting possibility about the veracity of the confession she allegedly made to Mrs. Buck and, in particular, the words attributed to her in the subsequent news reports.

154. *(Coldwater) Courier and Republic,* June 29, 1904.

155. *Detroit Free Press,* September 1, 1904.

156. Quoted in the *Big Rapids Pioneer,* September 1, 1904.

157. Ibid.

158. *Kalkaska Leader,* March 17, 1904.

159. Ibid., April 28, 1904.

160. The amount of Mary McKnight's loan here is interesting. Smith alleged that she raised the mortgage from $200 to $600 as a way to control the property after John Murphy's death and not, as Mary said, as a legitimate loan for improvements to the farm. If Mrs. Lightheiser's recollection of this conversation is accurate, then Jennie Murphy believed the $200 figure. One possible explanation is that Smith's allegation was correct. Or John and Mary made a new deal and none of their family knew about it.

161. *Hutchins v. Murphy,* 624–25.

162. Ibid., 624.

163. The Michigan State Court of Appeals did not exist in 1906; the Supreme Court heard appeals cases.

164. All accounts indicate that Mary McKnight first went to Jackson and from there to Detroit. Her prison record does not detail her movement in

Michigan's penal system. News accounts indicate Mary McKnight arrived in Detroit on December 18, 1903, although one story has her transfer occurring sometime in 1906. It is probable that she served her entire sentence in Detroit. The State Prison of Southern Michigan originally housed female inmates, but when the Detroit House of Corrections opened in 1861, the Detroit penitentiary became the state's primary facility for women. It housed some notorious characters, including Belle Starr. The Detroit House of Corrections also held male offenders. The prison contained two separate yards, one for female and another for male inmates, surrounded by sixteen-foot-high brick walls and watched from guard towers. A brief overview of Michigan's penal system can be found in Carlson, "Michigan," 1,101–04.

165. *State of Michigan*, 139–40. Belle and Sam Starr were federal prisoners convicted of horse theft. According to a Bureau of Labor report for 1903, the House of Corrections contained 438 prisoners: 372 men and 66 women. Of the 66 women incarcerated there, 37 were "from State courts of record." The remainder came from federal courts. The cost for feeding and clothing each inmate in 1903 was thirteen cents, and inmates were involved in the manufacture of chairs, brushes and buttons. Mary McKnight worked in the button department.

166. A *Detroit Tribune* writer estimated McKnight's weight at 126 at her trial's conclusion; her Detroit of Corrections prison record in the Burton Historical Library at the Detroit Public Library gives her weight as 133 pounds at or around the time she transferred from Jackson. It also notes that she arrived in "poor health."

167. Chalker's statement provides an interesting clue about Mary's mental state during her incarceration in the Kalkaska jail. She admitted to taking a combination of strychnine and quinine, but it is conceivable she was taking a combination of patent medicines, some of which may have contained powerful narcotics such as opium, cocaine and heroin. At the trial, Creighton said that he shouted at Mary because she rattled his cage, literally, which could indicate claustrophobia, stir-craziness or possible withdrawal.

168. Chalker's statement quoted in the *Kalkaska Leader*, February 11, 1904.

169. *Detroit Free Press*, June 11, 1903.

170. Mary McKnight's prison record from the prison index in the Archives of Michigan notes that Governor Sleeper officially paroled her on June 7, 1920. She was discharged on November 26, 1926.

171. *Detroit Free Press*, June 19, 1920. Mary's parole was delayed because Major Margaret Duffy, who agreed to look after Mary following her release, became ill.

172. Several newspapers ran stories about Mary's parole. Mary McKnight's statement quoted in the *Ludington Daily News*, June 21, 1920, and the *Detroit Free Press*, June 19, 1920.
173. *Ludington Daily News*, June 21, 1920; *Detroit Free Press*, June 19, 1920.
174. Harper, *Who's Who*, 106; obituary for Clyde C. Chittenden, *Seattle Times*, April 15, 1953.
175. Judge Gilbert's obituary appears in the May 1, 1950 edition of the *(Traverse City) Record Eagle*.

CHAPTER 15

176. Wakefield, *All Our Yesterdays*, 108.
177. Ibid., 109. According to Wakefield, James Murphy's wife, Jennie, once remarked "Mary liked to go to funerals."
178. *The People of the State of Michigan v. Peter Anderson*.
179. *Alpena Evening News*, June 12, 1903.
180. *Kalkaska Leader*, February 11, 1904.
181. *Detroit Free Press*, December 11, 1903. The first poll of the jury revealed seven for conviction against five for acquittal; by the second poll, it stood at nine to three.
182. *Kalkaska Leader*, February 11, 1904.

Bibliography

Documents

Michigan Department of State. Lansing Vital Records Division. Certificate and record of death of Dorothy Jenson, March 28, 1902. Certificate no. 16. Crawford County, Village of Grayling, Michigan.

———. Certificate and record of death of George Lechman, October 23, 1903. Certificate no. 191. Shiawassee County, Hazelton Township, Michigan.

———. Certificate and record of death of George Steward, December 3, 1902. Certificate no. 226. Mecosta County, Colfax Township, Michigan.

———. Certificate and record of death of Gertrude Murphy, April 20, 1903. Certificate no. 75. Kalkaska County, Springfield Township, Michigan.

———. Certificate and Record of death of Ida May Weisenberger, December 19, 1902. Certificate no. 359. Saginaw County, Maple Grove Township, Michigan.

———. Certificate and record of death of Ira Nicholas Wright, June 21, 1903. Certificate no. 183. Shiawassee County, Hazelton Township, Colfax Township, Michigan.

———. Certificate and record of death of Isaiah John Murphy, May 2, 1903. Certificate no. 77. Kalkaska County, Springfield Township, Michigan.

———. Certificate and record of death of Ja. Ernest McKnight, November 15, 1898. Certificate no. 23. Crawford County, Village of Grayling, Michigan.

———. Certificate and record of the death of Ruth Murphy, April 20, 1903. Certificate no. 76. Kalkaska County, Springfield Township, Michigan.

———. Certificate and record of death of Sarah Murphy, August 6, 1903. Certificate no. 79. Kalkaska County, Springfield Township, Michigan.

———. Certificate and record of death of William Murphy, December 3, 1902. Certificate no. 48. Crawford County, Maple Forest Township, Michigan.

The People of the State of Michigan v. Mary McKnight. Preliminary examination, June 1903. Circuit Court for the County of Kalkaska. Archives of Michigan Record Group 2011-42, Box 31, case 377.

The People of the State of Michigan v. Peter Anderson. Circuit Court for the County of Wexford, November 1903. Archives of Michigan Record Group 2011-42, Box 31, case 376.

Prisoner Index. Entry for Carrie Collins. Burton Historical Library, Detroit Public Library

———. Entry for Mary McKnight. Archives of Michigan.

———. Entry for Mary McKnight. Burton Historical Library, Detroit Public Library

State of Michigan in the Probate Court for County of Kalkaska. In the Matter of the Estate of Gladys Murphy.

———. In the Matter of the Estate of John Murphy, Deceased.

U.S. Census 1870. National Archives and Records Administration Microfilm Publication M593. Alpena, Michigan. Page 54, family of Isaiah Murphy.

U.S. Census 1870. National Archives and Records Administration Microfilm Publication M593. Alpena, Michigan. Page 1, Mary Murphy in Household of William and Sophronia Leach.

U.S. Census 1910. National Archives and Records Administration Microfilm Publication T624, Roll 683. Wayne County, Michigan, Detroit, Ward 7. Enumeration District 0100. Page 1A, Detroit House of Corrections.

U.S. Census 1920. National Archives and Records Administration Microfilm Publication T625, Roll 816. Wayne County, Michigan, Detroit, Ward 7. Enumeration District 557. Page 513, Detroit House of Corrections.

NEWSPAPERS

Alpena Evening News
Big Rapids Pioneer
(Coldwater, Michigan) Courier and Republican
Corunna Journal
(Detroit) Evening News
Detroit Free Press

Detroit News Tribune
(Owosso) Evening Argus
(Traverse City) Evening Record
Grand Rapids Herald
Grand Rapids Post
Grayling Avalanche
Kalkaska Leader
Ludington Daily News
Minneapolis Journal
New York Times
Phillipsburg (KS) Herald
(Traverse City) Record Eagle
Seattle (WA) Times
(New York) Sun
Toledo (OH) Sunday Bee
Traverse City Daily Eagle

Books/Articles

Bate, J. Victor. "Poison Plot of the Greedy Widow." *Headline Detective* 7, no. 3 (March 1943): 16–20, 46–49.

Biographical History of Northern Michigan. Indianapolis, IN: B.F. Bowen and Co., 1905.

Carlson, Jennifer. "Michigan." *A Social History of Crime and Punishment in America: An Encyclopedia.* Edited by Wilbur R. Miller. Los Angeles, CA: Sage, 2012.

Harper, Franklin, ed. *Who's Who on the Pacific Coast: A Biographical Compilation of Notable Living Contemporaries West of the Rocky Mountains.* Los Angeles, CA: Harper Publishing Company, 1913, 106.

Holstege, Christopher P. *Criminal Poisoning: Clinical and Forensic Perspectives.* Sudbury, MA: Jones and Bartlett Publishers, 2011.

Hutchins v. Murphy. Michigan Reports: Cases Decided in the Supreme Court of Michigan from October 1 to December 31, 1906. Vol. 146. Herschel, Bouton, Lazell: State Reporter. Chicago: Callaghan & Co., 1907.

People v. Caroline Collins. Michigan Reports: Cases Decided in the Supreme Court of Michigan from April 30 to July 9, 1906. Vol. 144. Herschel, Bouton, Lazell: State Reporter. Chicago: Callaghan & Co., 1907.

Powers, Perry F., and H.G. Cutler. *A History of Northern Michigan and Its People.* Vol. 1. Chicago: Lewis Publishing Company, 1912, 135.

State of Michigan Twenty-First Annual Report of the Bureau of Labor and Industrial Statistics. Lansing, MI: Robert Smith Printing Co., 1904.

Wakefield, Lawrence. *All Our Yesterdays: A Narrative History of Traverse City & the Region.* Traverse City, MI: Horizon Books, 2002.

Wheeler, John H. *The History of Wexford County: Embracing a Concise Review of Its Early Settlement, Industrial Development, and Present Conditions.* Logansport, IN: B.F. Bowen, 1903.

Yerrington, James M.W. *Report of the Case of Geo. C. Hersey, Indicted for the Murder of Betsy Frances Tirrell.* Boston, MA: A. Williams & Co., 1862.

About the Author

Tobin T. Buhk began his exploration into the dark corners of true crime when he spent a year as a volunteer in the Kent County morgue. This experience led to *Cause of Death* (Prometheus Books, 2007), an inside look at a morgue, coauthored with Kent County medical examiner Dr. Stephen D. Cohle. Their second collaboration, *Skeletons in the Closet* (Prometheus, 2008), details some of the more baffling forensic mysteries in Dr. Cohle's career. A love of history combined with a morbid fascination for the dearly departed led to *True Crime Michigan* (Stackpole Books, 2011), a criminal history of the Great Lake State; *True Crime in the Civil War* (Stackpole, 2012), a chronicle of the Civil War's most dastardly moments; and *The Shocking Story of Helmuth Schmidt: Michigan's Original Lonely Hearts Killer* (The History Press, 2013).

Visit us at
www.historypress.net

....

This title is also available as an e-book